Mary Cannon's Commonplace Book

An Irish Kitchen in the 1700s

To my mother, Marjorie Smithwick,
who did so much research the hard way.

To Alice Bouilliez, who illustrated the book
and took me ancestor-hunting in France.

Mary Cannon's Commonplace Book

An Irish Kitchen in the 1700s

Marjorie Quarton

THE LILLIPUT PRESS
DUBLIN

First published 2010 by
THE LILLIPUT PRESS
62–63 Sitric Road, Arbour Hill
Dublin 7, Ireland
www.lilliputpress.ie

ISBN 978 1 84351 185 4

1 3 5 7 9 10 8 6 4 2

A CIP record for this title is available
from The British Library.

Set in 11.5 pt on 16 pt Caslon by Marsha Swan
Printed in the UK by MPG Books, Bodmin, Cornwall

CONTENTS

INTRODUCTION

The Cannon Family: Some Historical Background   xi

PREFACE   xv

FFISHE

1. *To Stew Oysters*   3

2. *To Stew Eales*   4

3. *To Pott Eales*   5

4. *To Dress Cod's head, Turbitt etcetera*   6

5. *To Stew ffishe, Trouts etcetera*   7

6. *To Stew Carps or any ffishe*   8

7. *To Make Sauce for Pike, Mullett or Bass Boyled*   9

8. *To Fry ffishe*   10

9. *To Make a Lobster Pottage*   11

10. *To Make Forcemeat Balls of Lobsters*   12

INTERLUDE   13

To Make Plum Broth   13

FFLESHE

1. *To Make Alamode Beefe*   *17*

2. *To Make Scotch Colopes*   *18*

3. *To Make Scotch Colopes Another Way*   *19*

4. *To Make Forcemeat Balls*   *20*

5. *To Rague a Breast of Veale*   *21*

6. *To Make Veale Toast*   *22*

7. *To Collar a Breast of Veale*   *23*

8. *A Savory Sauce for Collared Breast of Veale*   *24*

9. *To Roast a Calves Head*   *25*

10. *To Hash a Calves Head*   *26*

11. *To Make a Calves Head Pye*   *27*

12. *To Make an Olive Pye*   *28*

13. *To Dry Neats' Tongues*   *29*

14. *To Make Mince Pyes*   *30*

15. *To Stew a Beefe's Cheek*   *31*

16. *To Make Sausages*   *32*

17. *To Make a Stake Pye*   *33*

18. *To Make Brawn*   *34*

19. *To Bake a Pigg in a Pan*   *36*

20. *To Make ffleshe Pudding*   *37*

21. *To Order Tongues and Gammons*   *38*

22. *To Force a Legg of Lamb*   *39*

23. *To Stew a Hind Quarter of Lamb*   *40*

24. *To Stew a Nick of Mutton*   *41*

25. *To Make Balls to Garnish Dishes*   *42*

26. *To Make a Frycasey*   *43*

INTERLUDE   *45*

BAKING

1. *To Make a Cake*   *49*

2. *To Make a Cake Another Way*   *50*

3. *Ye Countess of Manchester's Cake*   *51*

4. *Lady Southcott's Cake*   *52*

5. *To Make Almond Cake*   *53*

6. *To Make Curd Cakes*   *54*

7. *To Make Queen's Cakes*   *55*

8. *To Make Custerds*   *56*

9. *To Make Bunnes*   *57*

10. *To Make Bread*   *58*

11. *To Make French Bread*   *59*

12. *To Make Ginger Bread*   *60*

13. *To Make Sugar Cakes*   *61*

14. *To Make Cheese Cakes*   *62*

15. *To Make Poor Knights*   *63*

16. *To Make Puffes*   *64*

17. *To Make Naples Bisketts*   *65*

18. *To Make Excellent Wigges*   *66*

19. *To Make Bisketts*   *67*

INTERLUDE   *68*

FOR SUCH AS BE SICKE

1. *To Make a Sacke Possett*   *73*

2. *To Make Plucke Broth*   *74*

3. To Make Harts Horn Jelly 75

4. To Make French Barley Caudle 76

5. To Make Lemmonade 77

6. To Make Lemmon Water 78

7. To Make an Electuary 79

INTERLUDE 80

8. To Dry Eringo Roots 81

9. Eringo Crame 82

10. To Cure the Dropsy 83

PUDDINGS AND DESERTS

1. To Make an Orange Puding 87

2. To Make Excellent Lemmon Creams 88

3. To Make Lemmon Creams an Easier Way 89

4. To Make a Devonshire White Pott 90

5. To Make French Butter 91

6. To Make Chocolett Crame 92

7. Another Way but Slighter 93

8. To Make Almond Jelly 94

9. To Make a Guesberry Fool 95

10. To Make Orange Jelly 96

11. To Make Blancmange 97

12. To Make a Custerd Pudding 98

13. To Make Whip Sillibubs 99

14. To Make a Trifle 100

15. To Make Macheroon Bisketts 101

16. *To Make a Carriott Pudding*   *102*

INTERLUDE   *103*

WINE, ALE AND SPIRITS

1. *To Make Mum, as tis at the Town House of Brunswick*   *109*

2. *To Make Sider, Fine, Sharpe and Goode*   *111*

3. *To Make Lemmon Brandy*   *112*

4. *To Make Raison Wine*   *113*

5. *To Make Sage Wine*   *114*

6. *To Make Grape or Cherry Wine*   *115*

7. *To Make a Singular Guesberry, Damson or Black Cherry Wine*   *116*

8. *To Make Aprycorke Wine*   *117*

9. *To Make Vinegar*   *118*

10. *To Make Elder Wine*   *119*

11. *To Make Cowslop Wine*   *120*

12. *To Make Raspberry Wine*   *121*

13. *To Make Burch Wine (i)*   *122*

14. *To Make Burch Wine (ii)*   *123*

15. *To Make Burch Wine (iii)*   *124*

16. *To Make Methaglan*   *125*

17. *To Make Methagalan Another Way*   *126*

18. *To Make Methagalin, Mama's Receipt*   *127*

19. *To Make White Mead*   *128*

20. *To Make Black Cherry Beer*   *129*

INTERLUDE: *A Camel and a Crinoline*   *130*

PICKLES AND PRESERVES

1. To Pickle Grapes   135

2. To Pickle Barberrys   136

3. To Pickle Kidney Beans   137

4. To Pickle Oranges   138

5. To Pickle Cowcombers   139

6. To Pickle Stalks of Lettice or Purslane   140

7. To Pickle Samphire   141

8. To Pickle Mushrooms   142

9. To Keep Quinces ye Year   143

10. To Preserve Cherrys   144

11. To Preserve Cherrys Without Stone   145

12. To Preserve Damsons, Pears or Plumbs   146

13. How to Preserve Guesberrys or White Grapes   147

14. Another Way to Preserve Guesberrys   148

15. To Preserve Aprycorkes in Jelly   149

16. To Preserve Aprycorke Chips   150

17. To Candy Oranges or Lemmons   151

18. To Preserve Oranges or Lemmons Hole   152

19. To Dry Aprycorks   153

20. To Preserve Wallnuts in ye Shells   154

21. To Preserve Green Fruits   155

22. To Candy Angelica   156

EPILOGUE   157

INTRODUCTION

The Cannon Family
Some Historical Background

I have been familiar with my Irish forebears on my father's side for many years. Much information came my way when I was young and was neatly stored in my memory, which was extremely good. Not any more, I'm afraid.

My mother's family too was interesting, being first recorded in Ireland in the fourteenth century, but I didn't know much about it until I saw great-great-grandmama's Commonplace Book, as it was called. This fat, leather-bound volume, with its brass clasps, was intended as a sort of diary I believe, but my ancestress, Mary Cannon, used it for transcribing recipes. Wanting to place these fascinating items in some sort of historical context, my mother decided to fill in a background for Mary Cannon and her activities. She was partly successful and Google has helped me to fill in some gaps.

The Cannon family is ancient and highly respectable. Holinshed's *Chronicles* supply the earliest records of the family in Ireland in the person of Sir Hugh Cannon, Justice of the King's Bench, during the reign of Edward II of England in the year 1311.

According to Holinshed, he was '… slain by Andrew Birmingham, between the towns of Naas and Castlemartin in the year 1318'. No reason is given. It is as if, in those days, slayings were unfortunate but not worthy of explanation. A judge would of course have had many enemies. Thomas, probably a son of the slain judge, was later Provost Marshall (I have no idea what a Provost Marshall does, or did, but it sounds good). As I haven't access to Holinshed's *Chronicles*, I can only offer what my family traced, so the next entry is yet another Thomas Cannon, secretary to Sir Thomas Skeffington, Lord Lieutenant of Ireland in 1532. Arms were conferred on the family in 1614. At this time, the Cannons possessed a great deal of land in Norfolk and Pembrokeshire as well as in Ireland. Colonel Alexander Cannon is the next noteworthy descendant and I can only guess at the number of generations involved.

Now the Cannon family was Catholic, not having joined the reformed Church, so when the Jacobite wars started, Alexander Cannon, a professional soldier and a good one, was on what turned out eventually to be the losing side. He agreed to raise Irish recruits to join Lord Dundee (Bonnie Dundee of the ballad), in Scotland, but it was hard going. He meant to take a troop of 500 horse to Scotland, but with only fifty reluctant recruits, had to think again. He had travelled north with King James and tried to beg some troops from him, but the King was laying siege to Derry and refused to part with any. Colonel Cannon eventually collected about 150 mounted recruits, of sorts, and conveyed them across the sea to Inverlochy, in three French frigates. The weather was bad, so the recruits were seasick as well as being ill fed, ill armed and ill disciplined.

Lord Dundee was already preparing for the battle of Killie-crankie in 1689. Colonel Cannon arrived in time to reinforce him and the day resulted in victory for the Jacobites. It has to be said though, that the Irish troops were less than enthusiastic. Rounded up in a hurry, they probably had little idea who they were fighting or why. When attacked by the Highlanders who were as reckless as they were violent, the Irish were well boxed-in by Dundee's Scots. The Highlanders fought stripped almost naked, with their kilts tied up so they could run faster. They were armed with claymores and axes and raced over the rough mountain passes with bloodcurdling yells. No wonder the seasick horsemen were reluctant.

Although the Jacobites won the day at Killiecrankie, Lord Dundee was killed just before the battle ended and it was Alexander Cannon, a much less magnetic character to the Scots, and one who wouldn't have understood their language, who led the Jacobites the following day and thereafter. The armies engaged again, this time at Dunkeld. After a bloody battle in the streets, the town being almost destroyed by fire, the Jacobites retreated and, although Cannon had been promoted to Major General, he was faced with an almost impossible task: to convey his Irish troops back across the sea and leave Dundee's men behind. With 5000 Scots as well as the remains of his Irish battalion, Cannon did well to keep them more or less together. The thought of leading such an army whilst keeping it fed and in some sort of order is astounding.

One of my sources says that Cannon's men stayed with him because they had nowhere else to go, rather than from than a desire to fight. He marched them to Perth, Aberdeen, Banff and Moray, 'harrying the Lowlanders', and finally arrived at Mull, where he sought the protection of Sir John MacClean. Now 'harrying the Lowlanders' is a polite way of saying that they lived off the land, getting meat to eat by driving and killing cattle, and other necessities, by merely taking them as spoils of war. Cannon had left Dunkeld with about 5500 men and horses and no legal way of maintaining them. Return to Ireland was impossible once the Jacobites had been defeated and most of his troops were Scots. He was in a hostile country and the war had ended, with William III and his wife Mary governing Great Britain and Ireland. It's impossible that Alexander Cannon could have been at the Boyne. It was a tradition in the family, but must be untrue. Even had he made straight for the coast after Dunkeld, assuming that the three French frigates were waiting there – unlikely – he couldn't have got back to Ireland in time. The marches I've described would have taken weeks, maybe months. However, loyal Jacobites were welcomed by the French and formed the nucleus of the first 'Irish Brigade'.

I haven't found any record of Alexander Cannon's death in Ireland or Scotland for the good reason that he almost certainly died in France. I can find a record of only one child of his, a son, Patrick, described as 'gentleman of the City of Dublin'. And of Patrick I know nothing, except that he had considerable property in the city, but lived in Dun Laoghaire, or Dunleary as it was called until it was renamed Kingstown in the reign of George IV.

The Dunleary of 1700 or thereabouts was a small fishing village, situated where the Dart station of Monkstown and Salthill now stands. So small, that when the tide was out the bay was almost dry, allowing only small fishing boats to approach the land. Shipwrecks were commonplace, which was the main reason for the building of the harbour a short distance south of the village.

In the year 1700, Patrick Cannon married Mary, whose maiden name I have been unable to discover, and the following year, she started to write recipes in her Commonplace Book.

PREFACE

I was shown Mary Cannon's cookery book at my grandmother's house when I was a little girl, and remember only that it was heavy and smelt musty. I wondered why my mother was so excited by it. She asked if she might have it, but Granny said, 'No, it must go to the eldest of the family'. So Auntie Evelyn got the book, but not before my mother had copied all the recipes into a thick exercise book.

It was as well she did, as Auntie Evelyn died in a nursing home and the book disappeared. Some time in the 1950s my mother decided to type the recipes out on a massive typewriter, which bristled with keys of varying heights and for which she was unable in the end to get ribbons. A nasty, inky beast, I was glad to be able to sell it when it became an antique. The typed recipes were, if anything, less legible than the hand-written ones.

Mary Cannon wrote, one would almost have imagined, with a pin, so fine was the writing. The ink had faded to pale brown on thick, hand-made paper. Her spelling was reckless; the same word might be spelled in three different ways in one recipe. Some of the writing is almost impossible to decipher, owing to the peculiarity of the letters, particularly capitals, which sprouted wild loops and curlicues.

At the beginning of the eighteenth century English spelling had not been standardized. It was Dr Johnson who achieved this, with his Dictionary. I have retained the quaint spelling only when the meaning is obvious. Words which were baffling, such as *whit* for 'white' and *smal* for 'small', appear in their more familiar forms.

The archaic 'ye' is usually used for 'the', and 'them' is a 'y', followed by 'em', up in the air and small, like a date in a month. I can't reproduce this and don't really want to. Mary was economical of the space in her book, her lines close together and paragraphs absent. Her only punctuation was a full stop, leading to some bewildering statements until studied closely. I have inserted paragraphs and made meanings clear, but only when it was necessary.

There were numerous marginal notes, but my mother, hard-pressed to get the recipes copied before returning to Ireland and leaving the book behind, just noted down a few that took her fancy. This is a pity. I have included these along with extracts from *The Irish Herbal* (1735), a few old cookbooks and some notes by Nicholas Culpeper.

Patrick Cannon was a wealthy man. His house would have been a farmhouse of the type that doesn't get written up in picture books. I suppose they lacked romance. Earthen-floored cabins with a hole in the roof to let out the smoke were considered romantic by people who didn't have to live in them. So were the follies, well named, that adorned the gardens of castles.

In England, once Charles II came to the throne and the civil war grew distant, comfortable farmhouses and small manor houses sprang up everywhere. Life was less dangerous for a while. Once the Jacobites had been defeated, England launched into a life of pleasure and show for the rich, and comfortable living for the gentry. At that date, Irish people of a similar background were less secure and stayed in their castles. The few remaining farmhouses before the time of

Queen Anne were fortified with iron grids behind the window shutters, and tremendously thick and heavily-barred doors.

There are many books about Irish country houses, but nothing much about the kind of place where Patrick and Mary Cannon would have lived. It was probably plain and square and certainly stone built. Apart from that, I can only guess. Those houses I have seen that date from 1700 or earlier have been built onto at intervals, many acquiring ornate porticos or an extra storey.

Dunleary consisted of a cluster of just fifty homes. Mary Cannon would certainly have had a large, comfortable house, a cook; probably several maids as well. Milk, Butter and eggs were always plentiful and she was lavish with them. And the sea was close by, with its multitudes of *ffishe*.

FFISHE

I. *To Stew Oysters*

Plump your Oysters over ye ffire, then straine them through a strainer and save ye Liquor.

Then wash your Oysters well from ye Shells and putt them in a stewpan over ye ffire.

Putt in their own Liquor, a little White Wine, some hole Peper, a little Salt, ye juice of a Lemmon and some Anchovies.

Stew them till they be (*done*) enough, then putt in a quarter pound of Fresh Butter with an egge or two beaten up and sett into it.

Dishe them up with seppits round ye Dishe, with some fryed Oysters and Lemmons soused.

Seppits, also spelt 'sippets', are today more often called 'croutons'.

2. To Stew Eales

When your Eales are prepared for stewing, putt to them as much White Wine and water as will cover them, of each a like quantity and when they are boyled, scum them clean.

Then putt in a bundle of Sweet Herbs and three or four blades of Mace, a little hole Peper and Salt to your taste.

When they are stewed enough, Dishe them.

Take some of the Liquor and thicken it with Butter and pour it on Hott and soe serve it.

3. To Pott Eales

Take your Eales and skin them and cut them down the belly. Take out all ye bones and season first with Salt, then with a Rowe of Sweet Herbs cut small. Ye herbs must be Sweet Marjoram, Tyme, Winter Savory and Pennyroyal.

Then add a Rowe of these Spices mixt: Cloves, Mace, Peper and a little Ginger. Be sure to Bind the Eales and Herbs close with Tape.

Bake the Eales and after they are baked, take them out of ye Butter and while that settles, unbind them. Then putt them into a Pott and mix clarified Butter with that they are baked in and cover them all over.

You must lay some Bay at Botom and Top of your Eales before you bake them.

Bay berries 'comfort the head, mouth and nerves and are good against infections'. The oil would take away bruises and seven berries given to a woman in labour was said to ensure a quick delivery. Bay leaves are good in a hot bath to relieve aching limbs.

4. To Dress Cod's Head, Turbitt etcetera

Take water according to your ffishe and add to it a Pint of White Wine and same of Vinegar, with a handful of Salt and a good handful of Sweet Herbs and two shallots. When it almost Boyls, putt in your ffishe. If it be a Cod's Head, boyl it half an Houre, but if Whiting or Terbett a quarter Houre will serve. Drane your ffishe and dry it well upon coales. Dress up the Head with the Liver, Tongue and all that Belongs to it sliced and thrown over it. For the Sauce, take some of the Liquor it was boyled in with a little White Wine or Clarrett and two pounds of Butter if your ffishe require it. Add five Anchovies, some Horse Radish and sliced Nuttmegg, a pint of Raw Oysters, or pickled. (If pickled, wash them and take out only the full part sliced.) Add a Pint of Shrimps and a little Lemmon with the Peal. If no Oysters or Shrimps can be had, putt more of the Horse Radish.

Beat up ye Butter with ye Things above said. This is a Fitt sauce for any ffishe except Trout.

Horseradish prevents scurvy and relieves rheumatism and chilblains.

By the way, it is now known to be richer in vitamin C than either oranges or lemons.

5. To Stew ffishe, Trouts etcetera

Take some strong Beefe Broth, a Quart or more as your ffishe requires, a little Clarrett, a Shallott, a small bunch of Marjoram, as much Tyme and Cloves, a little Mace, a lump of Butter (about two ounces), some Lemmon Peal and a little Salt. Putt it in a Stewpan and putt in your ffishe. Lett it boyl a little, soe that you can scum it, then cover it close. Soe lett it stand and stew an Houre until your ffishe be (done) enough. Then Beat well ye Yolkes of three or four Egges with a little melted Butter. Take some of ye Liquor and Beat it with them, then pour all into ye pan, but first take out ye Herbs, Lemmon Peal, Shallott and Spice. Pour all upon ye ffishe boyling Hott. Soe serve it to ye Table.

Marjoram (oregano) 'is good for colic pains and disorders of the head and nerves, such as apoplexy, epilepsy and Migraine'. It keeps the devil away and was known as the 'herb of happiness'. It was also much used in love potions. In stormy weather, it was placed near the milk, to prevent it from curdling in the buckets.

Tyme (thyme) will improve eyesight and clear the brain. The name comes from the Greek word for courage.

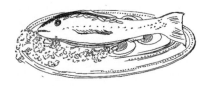

6. *To Stew Carps or any ffishe*

Kill your carps and rubb their blood about them and lay them in ye Stew pan. Putt to them of Clarrett, ale and water a like quantity. Then putt to them a little Mace, Cloves, hole Peper and a little Anchovie and Shallott. Then add one Onion and a little Butter.

When it be half done enough, take one Onion cutt in fine slices and fryed browne in Butter. Throw a little fflour into ye Frying Pan to the Onion and Butter and shake it well together that it may grow thicke. Pour your Liquor out of your Stew pan and give it a boyl or two with ye Onion and Butter, then putt it in the Stew pan again and lett it stew for half an Houre. Lay large Sippetts in your Dishe with a little of ye Liquor, and sett it over some coales that your Sippets may be dry. Then putt in your ffishe with ye Liquor it was stewed in upon it and soe Serve it up.

Sucking a whole clove was said to suppress the desire for alcohol. The natural anaesthetic they contain soothes toothache and they also have antibacterial qualities.

7. To Make Sauce for Pike, Mullett or Bass Boyled

Take some of ye Liquor of your ffishe with Vinegar and a few pickled Oysters, an Anchovie or two dissolved, a little Horse Radish and Shallott. Soe lett it Boyle a quarter of an Houre in your Sauce Pan, then putt in a good quantity of Fresh Butter and keep it constantly stiring until it be melted. When your ffishe is well dryed, Dishe it and throw ye Sauce over it.

8. *To Fry ffishe*

Dry your ffishe very well and putt it into your Frying Pan with a good quantity of Basting Suett. Flour it first and soe putt it in your Pan. When it Boyls up, if it be full enough to Boyl over ye ffishe, you need not turn them. When it is (done) enough, take them out with a skimmer and draine in a Cullendar and putt them into a Dishe that is not too Warme. Make your sauce of beaten Butter, two spoonfulls of White Wine or Clarrett, Nuttmegg and Lemmon Peal. If you fry Whitings, you must Beat them first to harden them.

9. To Make a Lobster Pottage

Bone six Lobsters and take all ye Meat out of ye shells and pound them in a Mortar, all to a puffle. Then putt them in a clean Stew Pan over ye ffire and add to it two Quarts of Crame and four Quarts of water. Season it with a little Clove, Mace and Salt, some Spinage and Spare Mint chopt grossly and some Forcemeat balls made of Lobster. Sett it to stew over ye ffire, then cutt two Loafs of French Bread in square Bitts and putt into ye Pottage with one pound of Fresh Butter. When it is (done) enough, Garnish ye Dishe with ye Claws of ye Lobsters and Serve it.

Spinage 'applied externally, dissolves inflammatory tumours and boils'.

Spare Mint is spearmint. Mint was named for Minthe, a nymph turned into a plant, as so many were, by the Gods.

10. To Make Forcemeat Balls of Lobsters

Pound ye Meat of one Lobster with as muche Fresh Butter as Meat. Season it with a little Peper, Cloves, Mace and Nuttmegs. Then add some grated Bread and ye Yolkes of two Egges, and make it into Balls and soe it will be Fitt for use.

INTERLUDE

One of the striking things about this book is the fact that there are so few recipes for soup and broth. True, there are a couple in the section *For Such as be Sicke*, although you get the impression that a Sacke Possett with its warming alcohol would have been considered more appropriate than a nice piece of steamed fish. I'm inclined to agree.

The only recipe for broth follows:

To Make Plum Broth

Take a legge or two shins of Beefe. Break the bones and make of them strong Jelly Broth. When it is thoroughly Boyled, strane it from ye Meat, then putt to it as much grated bread as will thicken it. Then to six gallions of this Broth, putt of Raisons, currans and prewens (*prunes*) of each two pounds, some cloves and mace powdered.

When the frewitt (*fruit*) is boyled enough, season it with Salt, Sugar & Sack.

A good recipe for a cold winter's day at the windy seaside!

A mixture of dried roseleaves, cloves and mint putt in a bag will cause you to sleep and is good to smell.

The fish mentioned are quite a mixed bag. Lobster, turbot and oysters are an everyday choice. Trout, eel, carp and cod are used and bass is boiled along with pike and mullet.

All of these fish except lobsters were used regularly and treated much the same. There is only one recipe for oysters alone and that is for stewing them. However, later in the book they are used as accompaniment or ingredients in a variety of dishes. Cooked or pickled, they were 'Thrown' or 'Cast' into stews, or were in the makeup of sauces.

In those days when there was no port or harbour there, the village of Dunleary was farther north than today's harbour town. Certainly there wouldn't have been any big boats calling there; the coast was too dangerous. Small fishing boats worked close to the shore, where they could run for shelter or even run aground if there was a sudden squall.

In her recipe for carp, Mary starts, 'First kill your carp…' so she must have collected her fish alive. Or maybe a member of her family or staff caught them.

Cooking over an open fire, stewing and boiling were the most usual ways to cook and there is just one recipe for fried fish, accompanied by a delicious-sounding sauce. Like many of her sauces, this contains nutmeg, which surely didn't originate in Ireland. Checking its properties, I see that: 'A sixteenth-century monk, well informed on the pleasures of the flesh, said that any man wishing to make the most of his youthful vigour, should coat a certain part of his anatomy with nutmeg oil, which would guarantee unflagging activity for several days.'

FFLESHE

1. To Make Alamode Beefe

Take a peace of Buttock Beefe. It may be some four to six inches Thicke and ye ffat taken off. It must be cut Round and Handsome.

Lett it lye a Night and a Day in a Pint of Vinegar. Then Lard it very well with ffat Bacon thrust through. Then you must Season it very well with Peper, Cloves, Mace and Jamaica Peper. Soe putt it in a Pott with a quart of Clarrett and as much Clear Gravey as will just cover it. If you want for Gravey, you may putt soe much water.

Then putt a bunch of Tyme and an Onion stuck with Cloves in and cover the pott very close. Ye best way is to cover it with a paste. Then bake it in an oven with Bread, for it must be baked very well. Then take it Nicely out of ye Pott and lett it stand in a dry Dishe and soe cutt it out in thin Slices at Pleasure and thus it is done for keeping Cold. If it is to be eaten Hott, you must take ye Liquor it was baked in and thicke it up with burnt Butter and Mushrooms and Hartechoke bottoms and Pallets. When you have shaked this Rague up together you must putt it over ye Beefe on ye Dishe and soe serve it to Table.

Tyme (thyme) 'pounded with vinegar, removes warts. Pounded with barley meal it makes a good poultice for sciatica.' Better still, it enables one to see fairies.

I discovered the meaning of (edible) pallets recently. They were pieces of pork chine.

2. To Make Scotch Colopes

Cutt your Veale sliced very thin, Hacke them with ye Backe of a knife, fry them over a Quicke ffire in Butter, take them out of ye Pan and Sett them before ye ffire.

Then brown some fflour and shake some Butter in it and shred a little Onion in it. Take some Oysters, Mushrooms, Forcemeat Balls, Pallets and Veale Sweetbreads and fling all this into your Pan.

Putt in Broth and Gravey and lett it boyl till it be Thicke. Season it with Peper, Salt and Nuttmegg, sharpen it with Lemmon, fry some rashares of Bacon and lay round it. Garnish your Dishe with Lemmon and Sorrell leaves.

John Evelyn thought that Sorrel imparted 'so grateful a quickness to the "sallet" that it should never be left out.' He wrote in 1720:

> *Sorrel sharpens the appetite, assuages heat, cools the liver and strengthens the heart; is an antiscorbutic, resisting putrefaction and in the making of sallets imparts a grateful quickness to the rest as supplying the want of oranges and lemons. Together with Salt, it gives both the name and the relish to sallets from the sapidity, which renders not plants and herbs only, but men themselves pleasant and agreeable.*

Sallets are presumably salads.

3. To Make Scotch Colopes Another Way

Take a Legg of Veale, slice out ye ffleshe from ye Sinews in thin(e) slices. Beat it very well with the Backe of a knife, then grate a little Nuttmegg over it, turning each piece.

Take four Egges and a little Salt and Beat them very well. Dipp each piece in ye Egges and lett it lye two houres. Then fry them in fresh Butter.

Have ready half a pint of Mutton Gravey, as much Clarrett, some Anchovie, Shallott and a little Nuttmegg sliced.

Boyl these in a skillet and when your Colopes are fryed, pour it into ye Frying Pan upon them and give them a Warme or two. Then laye ye Colopes in ye Dishe and pour on ye sauce.

Garnish ye Dishe with slices of Bacon Fryed, balls of Forcemeat, Oysters Dippt and Fryed in Egges and flat Clary Cakes fryed in Egges with slices of Lemmon if you have it.

Mary Cannon used shallots regularly, but seldom mentions the ordinary onion. Like onions, shallots applied to the skin are known to relieve wasp and bee stings. They have a list of medicinal properties, including a reputation for keeping cancer away.

4. To Make Forcemeat Balls

Take ye fleshy part of a Legg of Veale or Lamb, shred it as small as may be with a little Marjoram and Tyme, a little Spice and Salt and some Beefe Suett chopt small.

Beat two or three or more Yolkes of Egges and make this into a Paste. Role Round and Long and flour them well. Then Fry, bake or stew them as your Dishe requires.

5. To Rague a Breast of Veale

There must be two Palletts, four Neck Sweetbreads (to be Larded) one dozen of Cock's Combes, two ounces of Morells, some Mushrooms and two quarts of Gravey.

All these to be Boyld Leisurely until it be Thicke enough. Then add some Forcemeat Balls and Bacon, with Spice, Herbs, Lemmon, Anchoveys and Wine.

Serve up on a Dishe Garnished with fresh leaves of Herbs

6. To Make Veale Toast

Shred ye Kidney of a Roasted Loin of Veale very small and Mingle it with a Handfull of Currans, a few Almonds beaten with some Rose Water, a very little Grated Bread, a little Nuttmegg and two Yolkes of Egges.

Add to all these some sweet Beefe Suett. Then cutt off the crust of a Manchett and cutt it into thin Toasts. Laye the Meat on them and fry them a while. Then turn them, laye ye Meat on ye other side and fry them well.

A manchette is a lump of batch bread.

7. To Collar a Breast of Veale

Bone a Breast of Veale and Beat it well with a Roling Pin. Take a Handfull of sweet Herbs, *viz*: Tyme, Parsly and a little Sage and shred then very small. Have ready Cloves, Nuttmegg, Mace and a little Peper, beaten very small and mixt in Convenient Quantity with ye Herbes.

Then Beat two or three Egges and washe your Veale all over with ye Egges. Then throw on ye Seasoning and add a Sufficient Quantity of Salt.

Cutt some ffat Bacon into Lardy slices as Thicke as your Finger and laye them at a small Distance on ye Veale. Then role it very Hard and cover it close and Boyl it tender.

Cutt the Veale into four pieces and soe Dishe it up very Hott with a Savory Sauce.

8. A Savory Sauce for Collared Breast of Veale

Boyl ye bones of ye Veale and add to them one Nuttmegg and one Anchovie. Beat it up with a lump of Butter and some Oysters if in Season.

Sage if eaten 'can benefit pregnant women and can also promote conception. The juice, drunk with honey, is useful against vomiting of blood'. It prolongs life also.

9. To Roast a Calves Head

Boyl the Head till it be Pritty Tender, then take it and tie it up Fast with Filletting. Then Spitt it by a good ffire.

Take ye Braines and stew them well in Clarrett with an Anchovie, a piece of Nuttmegg, Lemmon and a Pint of Oysters with their Liquor.

Add some sweet Butter and putt it in ye Dishe with ye Head. Garnish it with thin Slices of Bacon boyled and Forcemeat.

10. *To Hash a Calves Head*

After you have Parboyld your head, picke it Clean and slice it thin. Season it with Nuttmegg, Salt and Mace.

Take a Pint of Gravey, mix with as much White Wine and boyl your Meat in it, with a Bundle of Sweet Marjoram, Tyme, White Savory, some Lemmon Peal, ten Pickled Oysters, three Anchoveys, two or three bunches of Samphire and a few Capers.

Putt this into your Stew Pan and lett it stew half an Houre at least. Then take ye Yolkes of two Egges, Beat them with a spoonful of Vinegar and a little of the Liquor you stewed it in. Cast it into ye Pan and Shake it Suddenly together that it may not Curdle, which it soon doth if Care be not Taken.

Garnish your Dishe with Slices of Lemmon, Pickled Oysters and Grated Bread.

Savory, a garden herb, is 'beneficial for the mouth, lungs and womb'. It 'eases flatulence, so is used in bean and pea dishes'.

II. *To Make a Calves Head Pye*

Half Boyl a Calves Head and cutt it into Small pieces, about ye Bigness of an Oyster.

Season it with Peper, Mace, Cloves and Nuttmegg. Add to it Balls of Forcemeat, some Lemmon, some Oysters, four Anchoveys, a few Capers, some Barberrys, a few Shallotts and some sweet Herbs.

Putt these into your Dishe and putt on a good Deal of Butter. Sett it in your Oven when not too Hott. Lett it remain until it be Thicke and ye Veale soft to your Liking and soe Serve it up.

12. *To Make an Olive Pye*

Cutt some of a Legg of Veale in thin Slices and Beat it well with ye top of a Choping Knife. Then chop some Sweet Herbs and mince some Beefe Suett very small.

Mix together some Crame, the Yolkes of Several Egges, spice, Sugar and some Salt with some Currans. Soe, role up your Veale with this collection and putt it into your Pye with some sweet Butter and soe bake it very well.

13. To Dry Neats' Tongues

Take Brine, Salt Peter and Salt and putt it into pump water and make it strong enough to bear an Egge. When it is cold, putt in your Tongues.

Remember to boyl your Brine once a week and renew it with a little Salt Peter. Three weeks will make ye Tongues Salt enough.

Take them up out of ye Brine and knead them as you knead Dough, very well. Then give them a twist or two in your Hands and pluck them out straight again.

Lay them on a Table board, or in ye bottom of a Tubb, where you can best press them. Putt a board upon them and press them with a heavy weight very well, at least forty houres. Then Hange them up in your Chimly a-drying.

The night before you Boyl them, water them in Pump water. One pound of Salt Peter will serve twelve tongues.

'Neat' is a collective term for cattle. Although archaic, it is still used. 'Neats-foot Oil' is used for oiling horses' hooves.

'Salt Peter' is now known as saltpetre.

14. To Make Mince Pyes

Take two pounds of Neate's Tongues, parboiled and Pealed and four pounds of good Beefe Suett. Chop ye Tongues and Suett very small.

Putt to this one pound of Raisons, one pound of Pruens shred very small, Cloves and Mace finely powdered, Salt, Sugar, a little Verjuice and Sacke. Heat a little in a Sauce Pan and taste it, soe that if you find too little of any of ye Engredients you may add what you please. You may putt in Orange, Lemmon or Citron Candid. When you make your Pyes, if you make of Umbles, putt in thrice the weight of Sugar.

Verjuice is a sour-tasting liquor, made from crab apples. Umbels are the heart, liver and intestines of a stag.

15. To Stew a Beefe's Cheek

Bone ye Cheeks and save ye Bones to stew. Putt to them eight Quarts of water, some hole Peper, some long Mace, some Shallotts, three Anchoveys, a pint of Clarrett and some Salt according to your taste.

Sett it over a ffire and, when it is half Stewd, add to it a good store of sweet Herbs, then stew it till it be (done) enough.

Putt in two Loafes of French Bread, cutt in thin Slices, stewing it a little Longer.

Take it up, then putt your Cheekes in ye middle of ye Dishe and pour your Broth around them, with Sippetts round ye Dishe.

16. *To Make Sausages*

To one pound of Pork, putt one and a half pounds of Beefe Suett. Shred them very small together. Season them with Cloves, Mace, Peper and Salt and some Sage cutt small.

Mix all very well together with ye Yolkes of two Egges and soe fill your small Mutton Gutts.

17. To Make a Stake Pye

Take a Neck of Mutton and cut out Bone after Bone. Season it with Salt, Nuttmegg and Peper and soe lett it lye an Houre.

While it lyes, you may take a lean piece of Mutton and mince very small with some Beefe Suett. Mince some Pennyroyal, marjoram and Tyme together and mix it with some more Nuttmegg and Salt, with a little Crame and a few Raisons of ye Sun.

Make your Pye pretty Deep and lay in your Stakes. Then make your Mince Meat into Balls and laye them into it as you please betwixt the Bones.

Against ye time it is baked, fry some Sage leaves in Butter and when you have cutt up the Lydd of your Pye, stick them in ye Balls and lay Slices of Lemmon between them.

You may serve it without a cover.

Pennyroyal is a common garden herb. It frees rooms of fleas and lice. Also used against mad dog bites.

This 'Lydd' would not have been pastry, more likely a paste of flour and water, to keep the pie moist and the flavour from escaping.

18. To Make Brawn

When your Brawn is killd, scald very carefully. When cold, Cleave it downe ye Backe without cutting a Chine. Ye Head and ffeet taken off likewise, as with other Hoggs.

Then you must take out all ye Bones throughout it, as clean from the ffleshe as you can. When that is done, cutt each side into four pieces. Lett ye Middle pieces, which are to make ye best Collars, be one foot or ten inches at least in Length. When it is thus, cutt it into eight pieces. You must have ready some water and Salt (but not too much Salt) and laye ye pieces into it for two Houres. Then take them out and with a Knife Scrape ye Skinny side very well. You must change ye water and Salt every four Houres for ye first twenty four Houres, else it will make it Red. You must Scrape each piece extremely well until it looks pritty White.

Ye second day, change ye water every six Houres and after it has been Washed forty-eight Houres, it will be Fitt to Collar. Then take out of the water and lett it Hang and Draine one Houre, then wipe each piece very dry with a Cloth.

Then Role it, beginning at ye Belly and soe Role it to ye Back. It *must* be Roled well, soe it may be as Close as Possible, wherefore the Men ought to do their Part.

Then with Filletting, bind round from top to Bottome as tight as Possible. Then sow up each piece in a Cloth very Tight and when it thus Prepared, lett water be ready in some Pott or Kettle and a little clean Reedes at ye Bottome.

Lett ye Collars be sett upright and lett them Boyl about six Houres, being putt in when ye water is Cold. When they have Boyled soe long, make a small Hole in the cloth and if you can putt a Straw thro them, then they be (done) enough, otherwise Lett them Boyl until you can. Take it off ye ffire and when it hath cooled one Houre, putt in a Pail or two of cold water to make it Coole faster. About two Houres after, you may take out ye Collars, which by that time will be a little Hardened and soe keep the better Shape.

Be sure to lett them stand upright until they be Cold. Then have a pickle ready of water and Salt, boyled with Bran and Rose Merry. Sture it whilst it is Boyling that it may not burn.

When both ye Brawn and Pickle are cold, putt them together, but first take ye Cloths from ye Collars, but not ye Filletting.

When Mary Cannon refers to 'killing your brawn', she means the whole 'pigg' or hogg. Pigg generally means a young pig or 'porker', while an older animal is a hogg.

The 'chine' is the backbone. You must avoid cutting between the verte-brae. 'Rose Merry' is Rosemary.

See too the next recipe, 'To Bake a Pigg in a Pan'. It would be impos-sible to find a pan big enough to bake a hog.

19. *To Bake a Pigg in a Pan*

Slit it in two and Bone it and Quarter it. Then take a Pan Fitt to Bake it in and laye some Butter and bay leaves in ye Bottome.

Season your Pigg with Peper and Salt as you think Fitt, with some cloves, Mace, Lemmon Peal and Ginger, shred with some sweet Herbs.

Laye it in your Pan, one piece upon another. Press it down close and cover it with Butter. Lett it stand two Houres in ye Oven. When it is Tender, then pour away your Gravey.

When your Pigg is almost cold, cover it over again with Butter and soe serve it.

20. To Make ffleshe Pudding

Take four pounds of Pork, picke it clean from ye ffat, shred it very small and mix it well with two pounds of grated Bread and three pounds of Lard shred.

Putt to it two pounds of Raisons stoned, two pounds of Currans, four Egges well Beaten, a little Rose Water, Cloves, Mace and Sugar.

Mix all this well together, then add a quart of Crame to fill ye large Gutts of the Bacon or Porker. Boyl them a full Houre.

You may Parboyl ye ffleshe, which if you do, then putt one pound of Bread to them and Boyl them three quarters of an Houre.

21. *To Order Tongues and Gammons*

Take ye legges of Younge Porkers and six Bullock's Tongues. Laye them in Brine, Salt enough to make it bear an Egge. Then putt a quarter pound of Salt Peter on your Gammons and Tongues and let them lye in it four or five days before you turn them.

After, turn them once a day and soe lett them lye until they are hard and firm, which may be in three Weekes. Then role them on a Board, which will make them eat tender.

When Mary Cannon says 'order' she means 'prepare'.

22. To Force a Legg of Lamb

Take a hind quarter of Lamb and cutt off ye Loyne. Then take ye ffleshe of ye Legg out of ye Skin (which you *must* keep Hole) and shred it with a good Quantity of Beefe Suett, a handful of young Spinage, and some sweet Herbs. Mix with these some grated Bread, spice, Salt and two or three Egges. Mingle ye Hole well together and Putt it all into ye Skin and sow it up and soe Roast it on a Spit or in an Earthen Pan.

Take ye Loyne and cutt it into pieces with what remains of ye Legge and fry it with some Fresh Butter. Then stew it in a little water, with Wine, Gravey, sweet Herbs and Spice.

When it is (done) enough, Dishe it up, putting ye Force Meat in ye Midst and ye Stew round about it. You may shred some Shallotts among your Forcemeat if you like ye Taste.

23. To Stew a Hind Quarter of Lamb

Joynt ye Lamb and putt a little more water than will Cover it. Take Spinage and Sorrell, a good Handfull of each, and six Shallots cutt Grossly. Putt them to your Lamb with a Crust of Bread.

Boyl it and Scum it and take it off. Then lett it Boyl gently until it be a Good Thicknesse. Scum off ye ffat and Season it to your Taste.

Sorrel 'is a laxative, cures ulcers, fixes teeth in gums, is good for the liver and makes caged birds sing'.

24. *To Stew a Nick of Mutton*

Cutt it into Stakes, cover it with water and lett it Boyl. Then scum it and putt in a little Peper and Salt, a Bundle of sweet Herbs, pickled Oysters, a half Anchovey and a few Capers.

Stew all these together about two Houres, then laye Sippetts in ye Dishe and serve it.

'Nick' means neck.

25. To Make Balls to Garnish Dishes

Take ye fleshy part of a Legge of Lamb and shred it as small as maybe with some Beefe Suett, enough to make it Moist. Putt to it some sweet Herbs, spice and Salt enough to Season it.

Make it into a Paste with ye Yolks of Egges, soe that you may make it into Balls and Roles.

You must Boyl them for a Hash, fry them for a Frycasey and for a Pye, bake them in it.

26. To Make a Frycasey

Take eight Chickens, Skine and Joynt them, season them with Salt, sliced Nuttmegg, a few Cloves, Mace and a little sweet Marjoram and Tyme, all sliced and Shredd very small. Mix all with your Chickens, then take a pint of water and two or three Spoonfulls of Verjuice or Sider Vinegar.

Putt it all in a Frying Pan and soe lett it Fry for a little While. Then putt in a Ladelfull of Strong Broth made of Knuckle of Veale or of Beefe and lett it Fry and Soake in ye pan half an Houre.

Take one pound of Leane Beefe, Carbonnard it on one side, flour it, putt that side down that is not floured, or Cutt into your Skillett. Putt with it a lump of Butter and soe lett it Stew a little while. Then putt in a pint of White Wine, a blade of Mace, some Lemmon Peal, hole Peper and Shallotts. Cover it close and soe lett it Boyl half an Houre.

Then take up some of ye Liquor and in it dissolve Anchoveys, making all Hott together and when it is enough, strane it.

Take ye Yolkes of six Egges and six Spoonfulls of Sacke and Beat them well together. Have ready some Oysters stewd in their own Liquor with half a pint of White Wine. Mix all together in a Stew Pan, putting in ye Chickens and Tossing together.

Soe, serve them up very Hott. Garnish with Gammon. You may make Rabbet Frycasey ye same way. Four Rabbets will make a good Dishe.

A 'frycasey' is a fricassée.

This last dish is the only one in the entire book that deals with poultry. Why? It certainly wasn't because hens were scarce, as Mary Cannon flings eggs into every possible recipe with a sublime disregard for economy. She must have had a lot of hens and, in those days, they were certainly free range and accompanied by roosters. This would seem to indicate chickens from time to time.

Perhaps the cooking of chickens seemed too obvious to bother with. Whatever the reason, 'Frycasey' is the only recipe she offers. But what a splendid Frycasey it is! It bears not the slightest resemblance to the chicken fricassée made of leftovers in white sauce that most of us remember.

INTERLUDE

There are plenty of recipes for meat dishes, not all of the Sunday joint variety. But Mary Cannon didn't despise offal and there are instructions for tasty dishes made from it. The most unusual recipe of the lot isn't contained in the list, because my mother couldn't believe the ingredients were correct. The instructions for 'Umbel Pye' seem very strange. This is the punning source of the saying 'to eat humble pie'.

'Umbels' are the heart, liver and entrails of a deer. No doubt there were plenty of deer running wild in and around Dunleary and indeed Mary must have cooked venison in various forms, although she doesn't tell us how. When a stag was killed, the umbels were the perks of the huntsman and umbel pie was a traditional dish.

Mary started off (having killed the stag) by advising the cook to wash the umbels and chop them and mixe them with 'good Beefe suett' and various other ingredients including raisins, prunes, verjuice and sack. Now comes the bit which, though clearly written by Mary's standards, seems extremely odd.

'For mince pyes,' she says, 'one pound of Sugar will suffice, but for umbel pye use thrice the weight of Sugar.' Three pounds of Sugar? Oh dear. I have included the instructions for mince pyes, but not for Umbel Pye as they are otherwise identical.

The recipe for 'Alamode Beefe' gives the first mention of 'Paste' – flour and water mixed, used to keep the goodness in meat especially reheated. 'Pyes' didn't mean something covered with pastry, but a collection of different ingredients cooked together in a baker or pot oven. Sometimes they were covered with 'paste', to keep them moist, but pastry was in the future. Indeed she once mentions the Lydd of a pie being cut up and removed, but this was probably flour and water paste, pretty nasty and very likely eaten by the dogs.

The vast majority of her meat recipes are made of veal, but studying them, I doubt if this veal was taken from young calves; more likely what we call 'weanlings'. There are just two recipes for adult beef – Stake Pye and Alamode Beef. Roasting was done on a spit, but the meat had generally been partially cooked first.

Baking would have been in a pot oven, or 'Bastable', familiar in Ireland over the years. Indeed my mother and I, many times great-grandchildren of Mary Cannon, made bread in a pot oven in an outhouse all through World War II. We tried to use the oven of our enormous black range, turning to turf and wood when coal ran out, but it was a disaster. The fire was much too hot and eventually burned right through the oven wall. A child at the time, I wasn't much interested in making bread, but always laid the glowing pieces of turf on the lid of the pot, with the little blacksmith-made tongs. Mary may have burned turf, wood, or both, and maybe driftwood; we don't know. I find it hard to get my head round the time that elapsed between Mary Cannon and myself.

These recipes were written almost 150 years before the great Famine, more than 300 years ago. When I first read through my mother's copies of the recipes, I was struck by the absence of potatoes and couldn't understand it. A hundred years later, they were the staple food of the whole country. But in 1700, when the first of the recipes were written, they had appeared in Ireland only recently and were despised as 'peasant food'. I have checked several sources about the vegetables most commonly used in 'great houses' and the potato is absent. A number of writers though mentioned the use of this new food for keeping poor people from starving.

BAKING

1. To Make a Cake

Take four pounds of fflour, four pounds of Currans, one pound of Raisons of ye Sunne, stond and choppd, three pints of Crame, one quart of Yeast ale, three pounds of Butter, eight Egges, half a pint of Sacke, a little Brandy and Rose Water, and what candid Orange Peal you please, with spices.

Putt in one pound of Sugar and mix all together with a light Hande and soe Bake it for two Houres.

Mary mixes in the Sugar with a 'light hande' but is heavy handed in her use of alcohol in cooking. I was surprised to see so much use made of sacke (sherry), Nantes Brandy and Rhenish wine. These were used every day in her baking recipes. Oddly enough, she doesn't mention the use of the wine, beer and mead that she brewed herself.

2. To Make a Cake Another Way

Take three and a half pounds of fine fflour, one pint of sweet Crame, one pound of fresh Butter, eight Yolkes of Egges and one White, and a quarter pint of Ale Yeast.

Beat your Egges well. Add a quarter pound of Sugar, two Nutt-meggs and a little beaten Mace.

Mingle your fflour, Sugar and spices with a little Salt, putt to your Egges a Wineglassfull of Sacke and your Yeast. Then putt it all into ye middle of your fflour.

Have your Crame and Butter melted and putt it also into ye middle of ye fflour. Stire in ye fflour, only reserve a little to strewe on it. Lett it stand warm by ye ffire for half an Houre, then worke it together and stir in three pound of Currans and a half pound of Raisons of ye Sunne, Stoned and shred small, warmed by ye ffire.

Before your Oven is ready, mingle in your Fruit and as much Suett, being cutt into Slices as thin as you please. Soe make it up into a Cake, cutt ye sides and lett it be high in ye Middle.

Lett it stand in ye Oven a little more than an Houre, then draw it, ice it over and sett it in ye Oven again one quarter Houre. Half a pound of Sugar will ice it.

3. Ye Countess of Manchester's Cake

Take five pounds of fflour, well dryed. Beat into it one and a half pounds of Butter as small as you can Crumble it. Then putt into it Ginger, Nuttmegg, Mace and Cinamon, of each a like quantity and all of it together one and a half ounces. Lett it be beaten small.

Then take half a pound of Sugar, four pounds of Currans well shred and mix all these well together.

Take ye Yolkes of eight Egges well beaten, a quart of Ale Yeast and a quart of raw Crame heated. When it is almost cold again, mix them also together, pour it onto your Cake and work it up as light as you can. Then Butter your papers and putt it into ye Pan. Bake it at least one Houre and a half.

To ice it, you may ye Night before, steep a pennyweight of Gum Dragon in Rose Water. Then, while your Cake is Baken, grinde it with a pestil in a stone Mortar and putt into it Musk and Amber-grisse of each one grain. Then putt in three quarters of a pound of double refined Sugar, spread with three or four spoonfulls of ye Froth of ye Whites of Egges and Rose Water whippt up with a Whisk.

Soe grind it about, always keeping your Hand one way. When it grows Stiffe, putt in a spoonful more of ye Froth and as soon as your Cake comes out, spread all over upon ye Cake pritty Thicke. Keep it neither too Dry nor too Moiste.

It may keep a quarter of a year.

'Gum Dragon' (tragocanth) is a whitish gum used in pharmacies.

Ambergris, derived from the intestines of the sperm whale, is much used in the making of perfume. Neither of these appeals as an ingredient in a cake.

4. Lady Southcott's Cake

Take four pounds of fflour, three pints of Crame, and one pound of Butter. Melt ye Butter and Crame together.

Take a quart of Ale Yeast, a quarter pint of Sacke, a half ounce of Spice and a half pound of Sugar. Putt ye Spice and Sugar into ye fflour. Beat six Egges very well, putt them into ye middle of your fflour and make it up.

Sett it a-rising by ye ffire. Take three pounds of currans, washd and dryed over ye ffire and while they are Hott, putt them into your Dough. Have a Hoop ready to Bake it in. It must Bake above an Houre. After it comes out of the Oven, strike it over with the White of an Egge, beaten with a great deal of Sugar and sett it again to Harden.

5. To Make Almond Cake

Blanche half a pound of Almonds in cold water, dry them in a Cloth and Beat them in a Stone Mortar as small as possible with some Rose Water.

Putt ye Almonds into a Bason with half a pound of Refined Sugar sifted. Sett your Bason on Charcole and lett it heat with continual Stiring till it comes to a Paste. When it is cold, make it into Cakes of what form you please and of what size.

For ye Sugar Plate, take ye Whitish Gum Dragon and dissolve in milk made with Almonds and Rose Water. When it is soft and Thicke, make a paste with a little Stone in your Pestil and cover ye Almonds with it.

You must take care to close up ye Edges with some of ye dissolved Gum. Then putt them on papers and dry them in a cool Oven.

6. To Make Curd Cakes

Take a quart of Curds, four Yolkes of Egges and two Whites, some Sugar, Nuttmegg and a little fflour. Stir them well together, with some Cinamon and Rose Water (if you like it).

Then Dropp them in a Frying Pan and fry them in Freshe Butter.

7. To Make Queen's Cakes

Take of fine fflour and Loafe Sugar of each one pound, dry ye fflour before ye ffire and Powder ye Sugar finely, then mix them together.

Take one pound of sweet Butter, wash it well with Rose Water, working it with your Hand. Then pour away ye Rose Water, but keep ye Butter, working it with your Hand, throwing in little by little ye fflour and Sugar till half of it be in.

Then take six Yolkes and four whites of Egges and putt them to ye Butter and then by degrees working in ye rest of ye fflour and Sugar. Add three spoonfulls of Rose Water and a little beaten Mace, with seven pounds of Currans, clean Pickt and Washed and dryed in a cloth.

Butter your Pans and fill them half full and sift some Double Refined Sugar on ye tops of them and bake them in a Quicke Oven for ye space of half an Houre.

8. To Make Custerds

Take a quart of good Sweet Crame and Boyl it with a blade of Mace and a very large Nuttmegge cut in quarters and a little hole Cinamon. Then pour it into an Earthen pan and stir it until it be cold, having putt into ye Crame the Yolkes of twelve Egges well beaten with some Orange flower water, a Quarter pound of fine Sugar and three graines of Ambergreece.

Then putt your cursterds into some cheaney Cups and bake them in an Oven that is fairly Cool. For in the care of baking, consists muche of the goodness of your Custerds.

9. To Make Bunnes

Take a Peck of fflour, two pounds of Butter, six pounds of Currans and three or four Spoonfulls of Clove and Mace beaten.

Mix all together, then take two quarts of Crame and heat it with ye Butter until it be Melted. Colour it with some dryed Saffron, dissolved in Sacke and Wett your cake.

Kneade it very softe and leave it covered near ye ffire about half an houre.

Then, make it up in Cakes or Bunnes, sweetened to your Taste.

10. To Make Bread

To half a Peck of fflour, use three pints of Milk, one quart of Yeast and four Egges, both Yolkes and Whites. Ye Yeast and Egges must be beaten together very well. Then Beat it again with ye milk and a little Salt.

Putt it thro a sieve to ye fflour. Then Beat it up with your Hands Light and when it is well beaten, lett it stand a quarter Houre. Make it up into little Loaves or Roles and bake half an Houre. Then Risp it.

'Risp'? I really have no idea.

11. *To Make French Bread*

To one peck of fine fflour of Red Wheat, warm one quart of milk and as much Warm milk mixed with it.

Take as much Salt as will season it, ye Whites of six new layed Egges beaten very well, a quarter pint of Sacke and two or three ounces of Butter.

Work it in your fflour and rubb it well together before ye Liquor be putt in. Then mix with ye fflour and make it into dough as Wette as you can worke it. Lett your dough lye a half Houre at least, covered and Warme.

Make it into little Loafs and putt it into Wooden Dishes. Lett it stand on ye Board one Houre more, till it be well Plumpt. Then sett it in a well heated Oven and bake it one Houre.

12. *To Make Ginger Bread*

Take fine Loafe Sugar, scearced and steep some Gum Dragon all night in Rose Water.

With the Sugar, make a paste of it. Season it with Cinamon, Ginger (finely scearced) to your Taste. Have ready your moulds and Dropp it into them.

Then shake it out on paper sifted with Sugar and dry them by the ffire. A littler Heat will dry them.

'Scearced' means scraped.

13. *To Make Sugar Cakes*

Take two pounds of fflour, one pound of powdered Sugar, two pounds of fresh Butter, six Spoonfulls of Sacke, ye Yolkes of three Egges, ye White of one and a Spoonfull of Mace beaten.

Knead all these together. Role a-board your paste and cutt your Cakes how you please and Prick them as Thicke as possible. Lett your Oven be heated only slightly, that they may not Loose their Whiteness.

14. To Make Cheese Cakes

Run your Curds very tender. When it sets, Break it and take the Whey clean from the curds. Let it dropp through a Range or else putt the curds in a Press a quarter Houre, then Rubb them through the Range with a good Quantity of fresh Butter.

Boyl Crame and thicken it with fflour to ye thickness of fflour milk. For ye quantity of twelve Cheese Cakes, take half a pound of Butter to Rubb them thro the Range withal, and soe proportionable to as many as you make.

Add ye Yolkes of eight Egges and ye Whites of six, beaten with Rose Water, Sugar, Nuttmegg and Currans, as much of each as you please.

Mix all together with your curds and fill your Cheese Cakes, putting them presently into a quick Oven.

Before you putt them into ye Oven, putt in each a Spoonfull of melted Butter. When they are coloured, they are (done) enough.

A 'range' is a coarse sieve or riddle.

15. To Make Poor Knights

Cutt two Penny Loafs in slices, dip them in Milk or Crame and laye them abroad in a Dishe. Beat three Egges with some Nuttmegg grated and Sugar and Crame. Then pour some of it upon ye Bread as it lyes in ye Dishe.

Melt some Butter in a Pan and laye in ye Bread, ye Wett side Downward. Then pour in ye Remainder upon them and soe Fry them. You may serve them up with Rose Water, Butter or Sugar.

16. To Make Puffes

Beat the Whites of two Egges with two Spoonfulls of Rose Water to a Froth. Then putt to it enough of Searched Sugar to make it Stiff as a paste.

Then dust Sugar on a Pye Plate, upon which dropp them out Round, at a pretty Distance from one another.

Bake them in an Oven not too Hott, as they will colour too muche. You may add what Perfumes you please and Wafers is best to Bake them upon.

'Searched', like 'searced', means scraped.

17. To Make Naples Bisketts

Take one pound of fflour Dryed and one pound of Sugar Searched. Then take ye Yolkes of ten Egges and ye Whites of six. Beat them well with five or six Spoonfulls of Rose Water.

Mingle them with your Sugar, beating all together in a stone Mortar half an Houre. When it is half beaten, you may putt in a Race of Ginger, clean Scraped, with an ounce of Caraway seeds. When all is beaten, you must have in readiness a Plate rubbed with Butter. Fill your plates and bake them in an Oven half as Hott as for Manchetts.

You must save a Spoonfull or two of your fflour and Sugar to strew on your Bisketts when you putt them in ye Oven.

18. To Make Excellent Wigges

Take a Gallion of fine fflour and Beat into it two pounds of Butter very fine. Putt into it half a pound of Sugar, half a pound of Naples Bisketts, grated very fine, a quarter ounce of Mace made very small and grated, Nuttmeggs and an ounce of Caraway seed.

Take three pints of Ale Yeast and mingle with milk a little warmed and mix all together as you do Cakes. Soe make them into Wigges and Bake them upon tinne Plates.

Prick them and just as you putt them into the Oven, wash them over with Milk.

19. *To Make Bisketts*

To half as pound of fine fflour take three quarters of a pound of Sugar, a Quart of Crame, half a pint of Ale Yeast, and a pretty quantity of Caraway seeds. Warme your Crame with as much Milk as will Wett your fflour. Knead it well and make it very smoothe and Role it into pretty thin Cakes. Pricke them and soe Bake in an Oven Hott enough for Taste.

INTERLUDE

The recipes for cakes, bread and biscuits are somehow different from those for meat and fish. These are all written in the same hand but for the most part in no sort of order. Evidently, Mary wrote them down as they occurred to her, or someone else gave them to her. In the original we jump from wine to fish to boot polish and back again. However, the baking recipes were all together, near the end of the book.

They have a touch of modernity lacking in the others. I wonder if the 'Oven' in which these cakes were baked was the pot oven with coals on the lid. I don't know how early wall ovens made their appearance in farmhouses. I have seen them in Yorkshire, used now as cupboards or safes, set into a wall.

If the Cannons visited their British relations, it's possible that they learned more up to date ways of preparing food. Patrick and Mary's only recorded son, George, moved to England in middle age and may well have lived with British relatives.

In the time following the Battle of the Boyne, when the Jacobites had finally been defeated, there was a change in the attitudes of the Cannon family. It seems likely that they changed their religion to Church of Ireland, having been Roman Catholic from pre-Reformation times, when their forefathers worked for and with the English administration. When the Jacobites were outlawed and the Penal Laws in force, many of the Catholic gentry embraced the reformed faith with enthusiasm, not entirely for religious reasons.

Patrick in those days would have been marked as Catholic by his name, but his son was called 'George', which is as far as possible from Patrick. Mary Cannon mentions 'the House of Brunswick' in her recipe for that curious drink called 'Mum' and Brunswick was the abode of the families that produced the first four Georges who were kings of England.

If more proof were needed that the family had left the Roman Catholic Church, shedding its loyalty to the Jacobites on the way, George chose as his bride Diana Rouquier, daughter of Moses Rouquier, a Huguenot who had fled from the French army as a boy, made his way to Switzerland, and thence to Holland. There, he joined King William's army, which was fighting King James and the Jacobites in Scotland and in Ireland. I am lucky to have Moses Rouquier's account of his family's persecution and his own escape from France. He is an ancestor of Alice Bouilliez, who illustrated this book and who took me to see the dungeons where his father was held.

The following is Moses Rouquier's own account from the original, hand-written in French:

> I, Moses Rouquier, was born at Caderles in the Parish of St Jean de Gardomangan, the diocese of Nismes in Languedoc, in the month of November 1670, of Pierre Rouquier and Jeanne Bourdanier, whose house was situated at the said Caderles in one of our considerable estates. We had another estate in the parish of Byrole, which is opposite and to the east of the mountains of Briou where we had a lawful right and to the west, the lands of Seigure Vallescure. We had a farm called the Madans of Fagus to the east of Caderles. We had still another estate, St Croix de Caderles, in the parish of de la Salle.
>
> In the year 1685 and month of September, King Louis XII sent to us to desire that we should change our religion, which we refused to do, upon which we were driven from our home to seek asylum in the woods and mountains. My father was taken by order of King Louis and led (then aged sixty-one years) to the castle of St John de Gard and there putt into a cell where he could not stand upright. There he suffered several tortures to oblige him to change his religion, which he refused to do. His sufferings were then augmented. He was conducted to Montpellier and from thence to Aigue Morte, where his miseries ended in the Tower of Constance, at which time I

was fifteen years of age. My brother Louis, whom I lost in the woods when pursued by the Dragoons, was only ten.

I was a fugitive with Louis for two years, until August 24th 1687, when I fled from France without having committed any act against my king or country, except adhering to the religion in which I was born and brought up. The Dragoons fired at us several times. I escaped into Switzerland and from thence to Frankfurt and Holland. I afterwards returned to Germany in the hope of joining there Malbos, the intimate friend of my father, but he being in Berlin I was obliged to stop at Vezel during the winter. In this city, the good God procured me friends, who represented my deplorable condition to the magistrates, who allowed me a reasonable pension each week to support me genteelly. On 15th April 1688, aged 17 years, I entered as a volunteer in the army of the Elector of Brandenburg, in the regiment of old Prince Holstein. In it I served three years in the wars of Germany and Flanders. The siege of Bonn was one of our most rude campaigns, for we were five months before the city, which at last surrendered to the Prince of Brandenburg after having been almost destroyed by our artillery. There remained only one house entire. Of 50,000 effective men, we lost 5,000 at this siege. I then accompanied King William to Ireland and served with him until the end of the campaign, when I had attained the rank of Colonel.

Sadly, I have been unable to find out who Moses Rouquier married, although I know he married in Dublin. In addition to Diana, who married George Cannon, he had another daughter, Alice, and a son, Moses. This Moses became a senior Canon of St Patrick's Cathedral, known as a Prebendary and Vicar of Howth.

FOR SUCH AS BE SICKE

1. *To Make a Sacke Possett*

Beat ye Yolkes of twelve Egges and ye Whites of ten, sweaten it to your taste, then putt to it half a pint of Sacke and heat it all together, then straine it.

Afterwards, make it Boyling Hott again, stiring all the while, then take a quart of milk from ye Cow and make it just Boyl, then stand it at as great a Distance as you can and pour it into a Bason, wherein you serve it into your sacke and Egges that soe it may froth. Keep it as Hott as you can with cloths, but lett it not come near ye ffire.

You may putt in what spice you please.

2. To Make Plucke Broth

Take a scragg of Mutton, a knuckle of veal, half a calf's tongue and a few Peper corns.

Putt to it six pints of water and Boyl it till it be but three.

Let the sicke person take a small cupful twice a day: thrice if the stomach will take it. Increase the Amount as you think best. It should be taken Fasting.

3. To Make Harts Horn Jelly

Take a quarter pound of Harts Horn. Cover and close it in a Pipkin with three quarts of water and sett it all Night in the Embers.

If it be hard the next Morning, strain it out and when cold putt it into a skillett. To three pints of ye jelly, putt a quart of Rennish and some Nuttmegg and Cinnamon; then Beat ye Whites of six or seven Egges and putt them into your Jelly. Stir them well together, putt it on ye ffire again and sweaten it to your taste.

When it Boyls, putt in ye juice of two or three Lemmons and Run it through a Jelly Bagg till it is clear to your liking. If you would colour it, steep some Concheneel in water and putt in that water as you effect ye Colour.

Hartshorn was just that. The hart is a male red deer and hartshorn jelly was given in the treatment of diarrhoea. Hartshorn is defined as an ammoniate substance, obtained from shavings of the horns of a hart. This was used to revive swooning ladies as, like smelling salts, it had a strong smell of ammonia.

'Concheneel', or Cochineal, is a red dye, derived from the dried bodies of a Mexican insect.

A 'pipkin' is an earthenware pot or pan. 'Rhenish' or 'Rennish' is a red wine from the Rhine and surrounding areas. One would think that, with all the 'gallions' of home brew that Mary Cannon made each year, she wouldn't have needed to keep Rhenish wine for cooking.

4. To Make French Barley Caudle

Take a quarter pound of French Barley, wash it very clean and Boyl it several waters, not less than three. In ye last water, Boyl it very well.

To a quart of this, take a quart of Rhenish and lett them Boyl together. Then putt in the Yolkes of ten Egges, well Beaten and sweetened. Boyl it to what thicknesse you please, always stiring it that the Egges do not Curdle.

Putt into it the juice of a Lemmon, some of the Peal and a blade or two of Mace. Sett it on ye ffire again still stiring it. When it is thicke enough, have some Toasts of French bread layd in ye bottom of a Dishe, in which serve it up warm. Putt in ye mace with ye wine.

5. To Make Lemmonade

Pare six large Lemmons as thin as Possible. Putt in five pints of boiling water and one pound of Sugar. Soe lett it stand all Day.

When cold, add the Juice of twelve Lemmons and three Oranges. Make it in the morning and lett it stand until wanted, then pour it out.

6. To Make Lemmon Water

Take the Rindes of one and a half dozen of Lemmons, Paired very thin and Steep them in a Quart of the best Nantes Brandy five days.

Add a Quart of Sacke and distill it in a Rose Still, covered close and keep a soft ffire under it.

Lett it Drop on Double Refine Sugar. You may draw two Quarts and mix it together if you please.

To make it more Pleasant, Clarify it with the White of an Egge. Add three ounces of Double Refine Sugar to each Quart and hang some Musk and Ambergrease in the Bottles. Make Orange water the same way.

Nantes is a city in north-western France, and gives its name to a popular Brandy.

7. To Make an Electuary

Take two ounces of filings of iron, of leaves of Rue and Aniseed powdered, each a half ounce. Add to them sufficient Honey to make an Electuary of a good thicknesse. The dose is a quarter of an ounce thrice daily.

The Filings of Iron Must be free from Ruste. This is Important.

These are the only under-linings in the book and the thread-thin nib has almost gone through the thick handmade paper.

One can see why it was important. This recipe has baffled me, as according to the dictionary, an Electuary is a sweet paste to be used to disguise the unpleasant flavour of medicine. But here the medicine would appear to be the iron filings – an extreme form of treatment for anaemia, perhaps.

Rue, sometimes called 'Herb of Grace' isn't tasty either and has an unpleasant smell. In an ointment it is good for gout and it used to be thought to avert the Black Death. As for aniseed, its medicinal qualities are well known, as is its distinctive smell. I feel that a large quantity of honey must have been needed.

INTERLUDE

There are two recipes in the original book that involve Exingo roots. Exingo jelly was a dessert of sorts, but the name baffled my mother and me. Neither dictionary nor encyclopaedia could help and, four decades later, neither could Google.

However, I think this problem has been solved by *An Irish Herbal*. This invaluable little book tells us that the root of Eringo, or Sea Holly, will cure most things.

The root 'provokes urination and menstruation, it encourages flatulence and removes obstructions of the liver, kidneys and bladder. It cures colic pains, is good for the nerves and as a general restorative. It is also useful against cramps and convulsions, and is good for consumptive persons.'

Evidently, what looks like an x was just an r and the recipe for 'Exingo Crame' should be moved to the section for 'Such as be Sicke'.

Introducing them here as an explanation seemed useful. First, of course, you must be sure to gather the ingredients. I wonder who first thought of digging up and boiling the roots of this prickly seaside plant, usually called sea holly, and whether it was for nourishment or medicine. Experimenting with the roots and seeds of wild plants would have been extremely dangerous.

8. To Dry Eringo Roots

Boyl your Roots, pith and Peal them and laye them in Runing water for four days changing every twelve Houres.

Dry them in a Cloth and to one pound of Roots take one pound of Sugar. Strew some Sugar in the bottom of a Pewter Dishe, then putt in a Layering of Roots and so do once or twice. On ye Topp strew the rest of your Sugar.

Putt a little water to them and Boyl them on a Chafing Dishe of coales until they begin to Candy. Twist them as you please and dry them in a warme place.

A 'Chavendish of Cloeschafing' is a dish of coals.

This done, you can make Eringo jelly for the sick person using the recipe for Hart's horn jelly with the addition of 'Shavings of Eringo Roots', or you can make the pleasanter sounding 'Eringo Crame'.

9. Eringo Crame

Take a pint of Crame and a quarter pound of Candy. Take some Eringo Roots and shave them finely into the Crame.

Lett it Boyl a Quarter of an Houre, then take ye Yolkes of three Egges, Beat them with a little of the Crame and putt them into ye Skillett, stiring it. Boyl for a little while, stiring it and then sweaten it to your taste.

Pour it out into a Dishe and when cold, serve it.

The only medicine that Mary Cannon mentions besides the frightful-sounding electuary is a remedy for dropsy.

10. To Cure the Dropsy

Take one pint of English Gin and one ounce of Jallop. Putt it into a bottle, shaking it well, that it may be mixed together. Lett it stand twenty-four Houres, then it will be Fitt for use.

Take a Glass each morning for three mornings, rest three mornings, then again take a Glassfull three mornings and pursue it to the Nature of the case. Desist when Cured.

Burdock roots made into tea and drank constantly cured a 'Woman of Dropsy that had been twice Tapped'.

   To be 'tapped' is to be bled.

   A 'Jallop' or 'Jalap' is a purgative drug.

PUDDINGS AND DESERTS

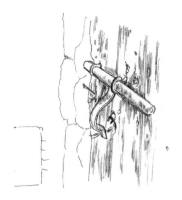

I. *To Make an Orange Pudding*

Take several Oranges, cut off ye end of them, take out ye Meat but not clean, soke them in cold water four days, changing ye water often. Then Boyl them in clean water till they be Tender, take up and clean a little within and soe lett them draine a little while.

Then take a good Quantity of Sugar clarified and make a Sirrop, and Boyl ye Oranges in ye Syrrop an Houre or more as you think good, till they be somewhat clear, turning them often. When they are Ready, putt them into a silver or Earthen Bason, then blanch a quantity of Almonds and dry them in a Cloth. Beat them in a stone Mortar with a little Rose Water in which Ambergris has been steept, then mingle with your Almonds with a little scalded Crame, a little grated bread, some crumbs of Marrow and a little of the Sirrop of your Oranges. Then fill your Oranges with it and putt them into an Earthen pan and soe sett them into your Oven (when the fervent heat is past).

Serve them up as you please, either in a Dishe or a Tart made for that purpose.

'Crumbs of marrow' seem out of place, whether animal or vegetable.

2. To Make Excellent Lemmon Creams

Take a pint of the Juice of Lemmons, a quart of water, a pound and a quarter of Double Refined Sugar, three or four slices of Lemmon peal, ye Whites of four Egges well beaten, with one deep Yolke, else it will not be Yellow enough.

Mix all these well together when cold, then sett it over a soft ffire, where it must not Boyl, it being very apt to Curdle.

Lett it continue over ye ffire till it be thicke and smooth, wherefore keep always stiring of it and when it is soe, take it off and take out ye Lemmon peal.

Dishe it and when it is nearly cold, scrape a little Sugar over it and serve it when cold.

3. To Make Lemmon Creams an Easier Way

Take a Quart of Raw Crame and Boyl it with a little Mace and Lemmon peal. Sweaten it to your taste, then take ye Whites of three or four Egges, beaten very well, and thicken ye Crame with them.

Then take of the Juice of Lemmon as much as will give it a taste, but not to turn it. Stir it a little over ye ffire and soe Dishe it and when cold serve it up.

4. To Make a Devonshire White Pott

Take a Quart of Raw Crame and Boyl it. Then Beat ye Yolkes of six Egges into it and putt into it a blade or two of Mace and sweaten it with Sugar. Then Butter a Dishe and slice into it some Bread and one Handfull of Raisons stoned and a good quantity of Marrow and lay on ye bread.

Pour on ye Crame and soe lett it stand a little before you putt it into ye Oven. Bake it not above one Houre at most.

Lay paste on ye brims of ye Dishe. Putt a little fine Sugar over it when Dished.

5. To Make French Butter

Take eight Egges and Boyl them hard. Take a quarter pound of fresh Butter out of ye Churn without Salt. Rubb ye Butter and Egges very well together till ye Egges be Soft (you must do it when ye Egges be hott) and sweaten with Double Refined Sugar, sifted to your own Pallett.

Putt in a little Rose Water and orange fflour water. Mix some Ambergreece with it and after that, rub it through a Cullinder.

6. To Make Chocolett Crame

Take a pint of raw Crame, Boyl it in a Skillett, then putt to it two Spoonfulls of Chocolett, finely grated.

When it hath Boyled a Little while, add ye Yolkes of two Egges, well beaten with Loaf Sugar, as muche as will Sweaten it and a little cold Crame to keep ye Egges from Turning.

As soon as it Boyls, take it from ye ffire and Mill it till it Froths well. Then putt it in ye dishes you serve it in.

7. Another Way but Slighter

Take of ye Thickest raw Crame and putt in as muche Chocolett as you think will Sweaten it and Colour it. Then Whisk it up a little.

Before it is sent to ye Table, whip up some Crame for Sillibubs and putt it on it.

8. *To Make Almond Jelly*

Take one Quart of Hart's horn Jelly and a quarter of a pound of Almonds, blanchd in cold water and Beat with Rose Water.

Strane them, Beat them and strane them again, until you have out all the Virtue of them. Then sett ye Jelly on ye ffire again and sweaten it to your Taste.

Putt to it a pint of Almond milk, stir it together and when it is melted, Straine it into a Dishe. You must melt your Jelly Scalding Hott.

When it is cold, strew Sugar round ye Dishe and soe serve it.

9. To Make a Guesberry Fool

Boyl a Quart of Guesberrys to a Pulp. Then Straine them from ye water and Beat them till they be Tender.

With ye Backe of a Spoon, force them thro a Hair Sieve. Then putt to them a good slice of fresh Butter, ye Yolkes of three Egges beaten and a Spoonfull of Rose Water.

Sett it either upon Coales or into an Oven that is not very Hott and you must not eat it till Cold.

10. *To Make Orange Jelly*

To one pint of water, putt one ounce of Isinglass. Boil the Isinglass until quite dissolved, then putt in the Peal and Juice of six Oranges and two Lemmons.

Lett the Peal remain about ten Minutes, then add a quarter pint of Orange Wine. Boyl it till it is a Strong Jelly, strane it and pour it into your Dishes. Strane the Isinglass, also the juice of the Oranges and Lemmons.

11. *To Make Blancmange*

Take a pint of new milk, a half pint of milk and one of Isinglass. Keep stiring it over a gentle ffire until all be dissolved and sweaten it to your taste.

Add a few Almonds or if you have none, a little Rataffia will answer the Purpose. Add a little Brandy, give it one Boyl up and strane it. To make a shape, pour it into a deepe Dishe, that you have soaked in cold water, that the Blanc-mange may not break.

Take ye Dishe out of the water as you are going to use it and be sure not to pour in the Blanc-mange too Hott.

Isinglass was the precursor of the gelatine we know. Whereas gelatine is made from the hooves and horns of cattle, isinglass was derived from fish, especially the sturgeon. I can remember isinglass being used to preserve eggs in the winter. Perhaps it is still. Nasty messy stuff and about one egg in three was a glugger...

12. To Make a Custerd Pudding

Take half a pint of milk, three Egges well beaten, a Spoonfull of fflour, Nuttmegg and Sugar as you wish. Stir it just before you putt it in the Pott and Boyl it one Houre.

13. To Make Whip Sillibubs

To a quart of Crame, putt a pint of Wine and Brandy mixed, with ye Juice of two Lemmons, ye Peal of one being Grated.

Whip it up with a Chocolett Mill and as the Froth rises, putt it on a sieve to Drane.

Fill your Glasses half full with ye Crame and Liquor and pile ye Whip on top of ye Glasses as high as Possible.

14. To Make a Trifle

Fill the Botom of your Dishe with Naples Bisketts, soke them in White Wine or Sacke, then putt over them a good Boyled Custerd. Let the Custerd stay until nearly cold, then Whip up a nice Sillibub and as ye Froth rises, putt in on ye Custerd.

The Higher it is, the better your Trifle will look. You may Garnish it by strewing Harlequins on ye Topp.

15. *To Make Macheroon Bisketts*

Laye your Almonds in water all night, then Blanche them and take their weight in Sugar. Beat you Almonds very small in a Mortar, putt your Sugar to them and Beat them well together.

Putt of the Froth of Whites of Egges enough to make it dropp into Cakes of what size you please.

Dust them with Sugar and soe Bake them upon Wafers. Then rubb them with fresh Butter.

16. To Make a Carriott Pudding

Take a stale two penny Loafe and grate it. Mingle it well with half as much Raw Carriotts grated, eight Yolkes and four Whites of Egges well beaten, Rose Water, Sugar, two grated Nuttmeggs and Crame. When you putt it in ye Dishe you bake it in, putt in half a pound of Melted Butter, stir well and soe bake it.

(This recipe appears in Colman Andrews book, The Country Cooking of Ireland, *and is acknowledged by him).*

INTERLUDE

(i)

I was surprised at first by the number and richness of Mary Cannon's puddings and desserts. Then I remembered eighteenth-century paintings of parties, from reverential pictures of royal banquets, to the gluttony depicted by Hogarth. Jellies were hugely popular and so were any desserts involving quantities of Crame, eggs and wine or brandy.

Weight-watching hadn't been invented and cholesterol hadn't been discovered. People occasionally tumbled off their chairs and died during a meal – if they were rich enough for that kind of thing – and their deaths were putt down to apoplexy, or heating of the blood.

Elaborate desserts were in vogue in the eighteenth century. As Horace Walpole wrote in 1750:

> All the geniuses of the age are employed in designing new plans for
> dessert. Gardens, architecture and pastoral scenes were evoked firstly
> in Sugar and then in porcelain to provide a backdrop for the fresh
> and sugared fruits, sweetmeats, jams, jellies and creams.

Sometimes such excesses overwhelmed the guests as was the case with a dessert table prepared by the Duke and Duchess of Norfolk, as described by William Farington in 1756:

> 'After a very Elligant Dinner of a great many dishes … the Table was
> Prepar'd for Dessert which was a Beautiful Park, round the Edge was
> a Plantation of Flowering Shrubs, and in the middle a Fine piece of
> water with Dolphins Spouting out water, and Deer dispersed Irregu-
> larly over the Lawn. On the Edge of the Table was all Iced Creams,
> and wet and dried Sweetmeats, it was such a Piece of work it was all
> left on the Table till we went to Coffee.'

(ii)

In the late 1700s nobody liked a big meal and a party better than Rouquier Cannon, the only recorded son of George Cannon and Diana Rouquier. He was well educated and popular, but unfortunately he was a gambler. He had seven sons and two daughters, but we don't know who his wife, Amelia, was before she married him. One of his sons, Aeneas, carried on the line. Aeneas fought with the Duke of Wellington in the Peninsular War and kept a diary. The following is an extract:

> My father, Rouquier Cannon was, I believe the only son of George and Diana Cannon. He entered the Navy and served with Earl Howe, but having some highly influential friends, who obtained for him some high Government appointment, he retired from the Service and settled in Dublin.
>
> There, being a highly polished gentleman and a great wit, he became intimately acquainted with all the distinguished characters of the day. Sadly, he contracted a passion for play, which survived his intellectual faculties and he became prey to gamblers who robbed him of almost every farthing. He died in Dublin in 1801 aged 61, leaving six sons and one daughter.

All my brothers were in the Navy and died or lost their lives in the Service. Alexander died of yellow fever in the West Indies, Andrew was drowned in the Mediterranean. Augustus, First Lieutenant of the *Eagle*, was killed in the moment of victory. He had succeeded, with the boats of that ship under his command, in capturing twenty-two sail of vessels on the coast of Italy in 1812.

Another brother, Rouquier, who was gallantly fighting beside Augustus when he fell, was immediately promoted to Lieutenant of that vessel and sent to the Brazils to bring home the King of Portugal, but died on the passage home in 1815. George died in the Service off the coast of Northern Ireland. I was born in 1787 and baptized into the Church of Ireland Henry Aeneas Cannon. In 1799 I became a midshipman, but severe seasickness obliged me to quit the Service. In 1801 I was putt to school at Mr White's Merrion Lodge Academy. In 1809 I entered the University of Dublin as a student in Arts. The same year, I studied Surgery and Medicine in the Royal College of Surgeons. In 1811, I went to London and passed into the Royal College of Surgeons and the same year became Assistant Surgeon to the Royal Artillery, starting duty at Woolwich.

I was ordered to Ireland and sent on duty to Athlone, where I made a much valued friend, Major Sir John Dyer. I returned to Dublin, to Island Bridge, under the command of General Wolff. In 1812, I was ordered to Cork to embark for Portugal to join the Duke of Wellington's Army.

Aeneas Cannon's diary tells us that he was at the Battle of Toulouse and returned in 1804 via Woolwich, to Dublin. In 1816 he was in Jamaica, in 1818 back in Dublin where a year later he married Emma Legh and the following year their son, Henry, was born. In 1821 Aeneas was posted to Canada and on his return in 1822 he retired to Dublin, where he had a private practice in Mount Street.

In 1825 he moved with his family to Cheltenham, where his wife had lived previously and there his other children were born, including in 1828 Mary Isobel Rouquier. His sons, all educated in England, did well either in medicine or in the army.

Emma Legh, Aeneas' wife, was a member of a rich and influential English family. Her home was Lyme Park, a colossal Italianate mansion in Cheshire. It's still there and was used in the film of *Pride and Prejudice*. Mr Darcy lived there. Aeneas was the last of my forebears to have the name of Cannon, but the name 'Rouquier' later pronounced 'Rokier', was given to many sons and a few daughters of the Cannons. Aeneas and Emma had several daughters, one being named Mary Isobel Rouquier Cannon. She was my great-grandmother.

WINE, ALE AND SPIRITS

1. *To Make Mum, as tis at the Town House of Brunswick*

To make: A vessel containing thirty-six Gallions of water must first be boyled, to the consumption of a third part at least. Lett it then be brewed according to art with seven bushells of Wheat Malt, one bushell of Oat Malt and one Bushell of Ground beans, and when it is tunned, lett not ye vessel be so much filled at furst.

When it beginneth to work, putt to it of the inner Rind of the ffir tree, three pounds; of ye tops of ffir and burch, of each one pound or handful; of Cardius Condictus dried, three good handfulls, of Burnett, Bettony, Marjoram, Avens, Pennyroyal, Elder flowers, Wild tyme, of each one handfull and a half; seeds of Cordoman brewsed, three ounces, Bay berry brewsed, one ounce. Putt ye Seeds into ye vessel when ye Liquor hath wrought a while with the herbs, and after they be added, lett ye Liquor work over as little as maybe.

Fill it up at last and when it be stoped, putt into ye vessel ten New Laid Egges; the shells not broken nor cracked. Stope it close and drink it at two years old. If it be carried by sea it is the better.

Transcribed by Will Richardson. Marchant
Doctor Hoffman added Watercress, 2 handfulls and wilde parsley, with six handfulls of Horse Radish rasped. It was observed that ye Mum with ye Radish was drank with more quickness than with none.

Don't try this at home! I'm assured that it would be seriously indigestible.
There is a saying that where parsley thrives, the woman is master. Homer recounted that warriors fed parsley to their horses to increase their stamina. It should be sowed on Good Friday and picking it in a thunderstorm will increase its potency.

2. To Make Sider, Fine, Sharpe and Goode

You must never suffer your Sider to worke, but stope it up Close as soon as it is tunned into ye Tubb. Keep a small Pegge in ye middle of ye Vessel and when it hath stoode four days or more, every Day draw out a Little in a Glass and observe if it be something Clear. If not, stope it up again.

When you find it something clear, then draw out three quarts of it, Boyl it over ye ffire and scum it. Then putt in three or four ounces of Isinglass, being shaved very thin and keep it on a gentil ffire, not Boyling til the Isinglass be totally dissolved, which will be in six or seven Houres. The Skillett must be Covered while the Isinglass is dissolving. This done, draw off the rest of the Tubb into a Buckett. Pour in the Isinglass warm and keep stiring a quarter of an houre.

Tun it up again and stope it for about two days. If it then be clear, as usually it is, or will be unless it is bad Weather, draw it off into Bottles which, the longer you keep, ye better will Drink.

If you keep it half a year in Bottles, you must putt two or three Raisons of ye Sonne stoned and a Lumpe of Sugar for it to feed on.

3. To Make Lemmon Brandy

Take two dozaine of Lemmons, pare them thinne, so no white be Pealed and Infuse them for three days in three pints of French Brandy. Then take as much clear water and lett it Boyl over a clear ffire with one pound of double refined Sugar. Then sett it aside until next Morning.

Then putt the Brandy and peals to it and run it through a Jelly Bagge several tymes to Clarify it. Lett it settle in ye Bottles before you use it and poure it off into another if you wishe to have it very fine.

4. To Make Raison Wine

Take two poundes of Raisons of ye Sunne, stoned and shred, one pound of Powdered Sugar, ye juice of two Lemmons and ye Peal of one.

Putt them into an Earthen Pott. Then Boyl two Gallions of water half an Houre and take it Hott from ye ffire and throw it into ye Potte. Cover it Close for three or four days, stiring it two or three times a day.

Then straine it out and putt it into Bottles and stope it not Close at first, lest they fly.

In a Fortnight it will be fitt to Drinke.

5. To Make Sage Wine

Take twenty-four quarts of Spring water and twelve pounds of Malagar Raisons, pickt and washt. Boyl your water half away and cool it again until it be Blood Warme, then putt in ye Raisons and one Peck of Red Sage cut small together.

Before it be quite cold, sett it a-working with Yeaste and soe lett it stand eight days, covered with a Blankett and stir it once a day. Then strane it through a cotton Bagg which you have ready, dipt in milk. Then putt it into a Rumlett with a pint of Malaga and lett it stand until it hath done working.

Stope it up and after about a month you may Bottle it with Loafe Sugar. If it should fly, you may open ye Bottles once a day to prevent ye Bottles breaking.

6. To Make Grape or Cherry Wine

Pick ye fruit clean and bruse it and lett it stand so crushed all night. Ye next morning, strane out ye Liquor and to one Gallion putt one pound of Sugar.

Stir it well and putt it into a Vessel presently, for ye Sugar being first stired in will make it work like Yeaste.

In a fortnight and three days precisely, you must Bottle it with a Knob of Sugar in each Bottle.

7. To Make a Singular Guesberry, Damson or Black Cherry Wine

Take two pounds of Raisons of ye Sonne, eight pounds of Powdered Sugar and four quarts of Guesberrys betwixt Greene and yellow. Bruse them into a stone Mortar pretty well. Mince ye Raisons small and putt them and ye Sugar into an Earthen Pott.

Have ready, when it hath Boyld a half Houre or more, two Gallions of Springe water and putt it upon ye Ingredients when it is yet Boyling Hott.

Cover it close, stiring it every day two or three times. When all rises up to ye Topp of ye Pott, it is ready to be bottled.

If you use damsons, you must bruse them between your hands, not in a Mortar.

8. To Make Aprycorke Wine

Take one and a half pounds of Loafe Sugar and three pints of water. Boyl these, taking of ye Scum as it Riseth.

Then take three pounds of Aprycorkes, pared and stoned, putt them into ye Liquor and lett them boyl till they be Tender. Then take out ye Aprycorkes and dry them or preserve them. Then boyl in ye Liquor two sprigges of flowered Clary, which will give it a fine flavour.

When it is Cold, you may Bottle it.

9. To Make Vinegar

To every six pounds of ripe Guesberrys beaten, putt one Gallion of water. Then putt it into ye sunne or some warme place to Ferment. It must be covered with some Cloths to keep it Warme.

In seven or eight days, when all ye Guesberrys are risen to ye Topp, draw it clean into another Vessel and putt in half a pound of browne Sugar to Ferment it again. When it hath dome working, stope it up close and at nine months, bottle it.

Corke it well and keep it Warme.

10. To Make Elder Wine

Take a quantity of Elder Berrys, ripe and free from Raine or Dew. Picke and Bruse them and, to six quarts of juice putt three quarts of Spring water and stir it well together.

Putt to it as much Sugar as will make it bear an Egge, then boyl it on a quick ffire and scum it till it be very clean. Then cool it in a Vessel and putt to it that same quantity of Liquor and half a pint of Yeaste, letting it work over ye Tubb.

Tunn it in a Vessel it will fill and, in about five weeks, bottle it, with a Knob of Sugar in each Bottle.

11. *To Make Cowslop Wine*

To twenty-four Quarts of water putt twelve pounds of Sugar. Boyl it half an houre and keep it well scummed. Take it off and putt it in a clean Wooden Vessel to Cool.

When it is of proper coolness, take two large Spoonfulls of Ale Yeast and as much Sirrop of Lemmons. Beat well together and putt into ye Liquor and stir with a wooden boule. Then putt in your Cowslops, two full Pecks, only the tops of the Flowers and stir them into ye Liquor every two Houres.

Keep it covered with a coarse Sheet doubled in four to keep in the Spirit. Ye third day, putt it up in a vessel, flowers and all and lett it stand a month.

12. *To Make Raspberry Wine*

Gather your Raspberrys when they are very ripe on a Sunny Day. Wring out ye Juice of them into an Earthen or Silver Bason. Lett it soe remain one Night.

Take another Bason of ye same sort and pour out ye purest of it and if it be a Pottle, putt one pound of very fine Sugar into it. (Lett it be beaten very small.)

Then give it one heat over the ffire. When it is very cold, putt it into a stone Bottle and stope it very close.

Keep it in a cold sellar and when you use it, to a pint of it take a pint of good Canary wine with more fine Sugar. Mingle it very well and drink it.

13. To Make Burch Wine (i)

After ye Liquor is taken from your Tree, keep it not above a day or two at Most before you Boyl it. When you Boyl it, to every Gallion of Liquor putt in one and a half pounds of Sugar. For every three gallions of the same, putt in the peal of a Lemmon and about twelve Cloves. Boyl it half an Houre or better, Scumming it as long as any doth arise.

When you have thus Boyld it, take a Toast of Wheaten bread (it must not be burnt). Spread it on both sides with Yeaste and putt it into ye Liquor to make it work.

The next day, tun it up, putting in Toast and all. When it hath been Tunned for about three weeks or a Month, draw it into Bottles and after a Time you may Drink it.

14. To Make Burch Wine (ii)

To every Gallion of Burch Liquor, putt one quart of honey, well floured together, then Boyl it an Houre with a few Cloves and a little Lemmon peal. Keep it well scummed and when it is sufficiently Boyld, sett it a-cooling. When it is almost cold, putt to it two or three hand-fulls of good Ale Yeaste to make it Work, which it will do like Ale.

When the Yeaste begins to settle, Bottle it up as you do other Windy Liquors. It will in a competent time become a most Briske and Spiritous drink.

This wine may be if you please as successfully made with Sugar as with Honey. You must putt one pound of Sugar to one Gallion of water. Or if you please, you may Dulcify it with Raisons of ye Sonne and compose a Raison Wine of it.

15. To Make Burch Wine (iii)

To every Gallion of Liquor, putt two pounds of White Sugar. Lett your Liquor boyl half an Houre and Scum it well (you must allow Liquor for ye wasting in Boyling). Putt in your Sugar and scum it as long as any will arise.

After that, take it off ye ffire and lett it stand to Cool. When it is almost cold, pour it off and putt to it five or six handfulls of Yeast. Lett it stand three or four Houres until it hath a good head on it; be sure to cover it close while it is working.

Have ready your Vessel, smoked well with Brimstone and ye smoke stopt into it for some time. Fill your Vessel full, stop it up close and lett it stand three quarters of a Year at least before you Tapp it. If you lett it take air when it is making, it will not be good. The Burch Liquor must be drawn in March, or as soon as ye Sapp riseth. If it is well made, ye older it is, ye better. It hath been drunk at four years old in Perfection.

16. To Make Methaglan

Take six Gallions of ffair water, fennel, Parsley, Saxifrage, succory, Eringo and Rosemary. Picke all their rootes and lett there be of each of these two handfuls pickd.

Boyl all together till it comes to Five Gallions. Straine out ye rootes and putt thereto one Gallion of Honey. Boyl it and scum it clean and when it is Milke warm, sett it a-working with ye best Ale Yeast and lett it work twenty-four Houres. Then scum ye Yeast clean and Beat it together and lett it work as long again. Then scum it and tun it and stope it close. Bottle it up in due time and after three months, you may drink of it if you please.

Fennel used as an accompaniment to boiled fish, was said to 'consume that phlegmatic humour which fish most plentifully afford and annoy the body with'. The poet Longfellow wrote:

> *It gave men strength and fearless mood*
> *And gladiators fierce and rude*
> *Mingled it in their daily food*
> *And he who battled and subdued*
> *The wreath of Fennel wore.*

Saxifrage 'eliminates flatulence and cures colic pains'. Parsley was thought to be poisonous earlier.

Rosemary has religious connotations and is linked in legend with the Virgin Mary.

Methaglan, which Mary Cannon spells in three different ways, is a kind of Mead.

17. To Make Methagalan Another Way

This may suffice for Some but is less good.

Take water and Boyl it an Houre and a half. Lett it stand to be almost cold. Then putt in soe much Honey as may bear an Egge and lett it Boyl a half Houre.

In ye putting in of your Honey, putt in two or three Whites of Egges to Clarify it and when it is almost cold, tun it up. Hang in ye Barrell some Cloves and Ginger, more or less as you like ye Taste. Lett your Barrell be full and in two months it may be Bottled.

18. To Make Methagalin, Mama's Receipt

To one Gallion of water putt three pounds of Honey. When it is blood warm, stir it well with a Whiske. Boyl it half an Houre or better, stiring all the time and scum it very clean.

Putt in likewise, the Whites of ten Egges, shells and all, two hand-fuls of Rosemary, four ounces of Race Ginger brewsed, forty cloves and one Lemmon Peal. Sow it in a Bagg together and straine it thro a Jelly Bagg into several Vessels to cool.

Putt to it a pint of Ale Yeast and tun it into a Barrell ye next day. Lett the Bagg of Spice hang in it and soe Bottle it in due Course.

19. To Make White Mead

Take a Gallion of water and half a pound of Loafe Sugar. Take a bunch each of Bazill, of Marjoram and of Lemmon Tyme. Take a Sprigge of Sweet Bryar, another of Angelica and a little Lemmon peal. Boyl all together almost one Houre.

Then take a pint of Honey, Beat it very white and putt it into ye water. Give it two or three warmes, then take it up and lett it cool and tun it up.

Make a Toaste and spread it with Yeaste and putt it into ye Barrell with ye juice of one or two Lemmons and the Peal of one. Soe lett it stand one day.

Then stope it up in your Barrell nine days, at the end of which bottle it up. It will come to drinking in three weeks or one month.

Rosemary 'improves memory and is good for the head. Cures baldness, the Plague and bad eyesight. Secures loose teeth'.

20. To Make Black Cherry Beer

Putt ye Beer of fourteen bushels of wheat to one pound brewed with four pounds of good Hopps. Hang in ye Hogshead one ounce of Cloves. It should be March beer and when ye Cherrys be ripe, open ye Bung and putt in thirty or forty pounds of them, the stems being pluckt off. It will be Fitt to drink in one Year, but much Better in two.

The virtues of hops are well known and a hop pillow helps sleep. Less well known are their abilities to cure the itch. The juice, dropped into the ears, cleans them.

Honey (used in Burch wine and mead) would have been plentiful, bees having been kept in hives from ancient times. Lemon balm was often grown near the hives and has more than one connection with bees. The leaves, which were a nerve tonic and heart stimulant, lowered temperatures when infused. It was also effective against bee stings. The leaves were sometimes rubbed on the beehives to encourage the bees to stay.

INTERLUDE
A Camel and a Crinoline

Aeneas Cannon and his wife Emma raised a large family, of which one daughter, Mary, was my great-grandmother. I cannot imagine how they managed, or more exactly how Emma managed to rear such a large brood successfully. I have plenty of dates for Aeneas' travels as an army surgeon and, in most cases, Emma must have travelled too. Mary was one of seven girls and they had two boys. My mother wrote about her:

> She was an attractive girl and I remember her well as an old lady; her principles were as rigid as her backbone. She fell in love with Charles Sloggett, a West Country clergyman, and when he became an army chaplain, she went to India to marry him. The journey took more than three months. This was just before the Indian Mutiny in 1857. Their daughters, my mother Alice and her sister Mary, were born there in the year that the Indian Mutiny broke out.

This sounds as if the girls were twins and they were certainly born in the same year, but in different places. Mary seems to have been the older by about ten months, her place of birth being given as 'French East Indies', which tallies with Pondicherry, where the family was stationed at the time of the Indian Mutiny. Pondicherry had been a French colony and the British had taken it for themselves at the battle of Plassey (1757). Plassey is one of the battle honours of the Royal Dublin Fusiliers, while the French army attacking the British included the Irish Brigade, of which Alexander Cannon had been a member.

Crossing the desert near Ras Messaga

The Indian Mutiny was confined to the North of the country. The worst of the slaughter was in Delhi, Cawnpore and Lucknow. These places were hundreds of miles away, but the telegraph had been invented and stories of the massacre of hundreds of women and children must have terrified the British population. According to family lore, Mary fled from the Mutiny on a pony with her toddler, Mary, and spent some time in hiding. Actually, it seems that she was sent away to an area believed to be safe. It was in a village named Duphaia that Alice was born. Charles had stayed behind. Being chaplain to the garrison regiment, he could not have left it.

Pondicherry is on the coast and is now a popular beach resort. Mary had gone inland and remained away until the Mutiny ended. Then she returned with the babies, Alice and Mary, and rejoined her husband.

He was about to be moved to the Punjab, a much more dangerous area at the time, and it was there that she gave birth to Maxwell a year later. English children were seldom reared in India and in a letter she referred to the baby as being 'puny', so she set off by ship to take all three back to England. At this time Maxwell was a baby and the little girls were just two and almost three.

Today she would have sailed through the Suez Canal, but she was years too soon. As there was no canal there, she had to cross the Sinai desert on a camel with her three infants. I'd love to know how long it took and how they managed. Not surprisingly, there was a five year gap before she had another child.

Great-grandmother seldom referred to these events, but when my mother asked her how she rode a camel such distance, with three babies and in baking heat she replied, 'It had to be.' She paused. 'My crinoline was a nuisance.'

PICKLES AND PRESERVES

In the early eighteenth century and for a long time thereafter, it must have been a nightmare trying to preserve food for the winter months.

Hard as it was to keep food fresh in warm weather, it must have been even worse trying to get the summer fruits and vegetables gathered, then pickled, candied or dried, so as to keep a family fed later on.

Even worse was the pressing need to pickle Meat. Once killed, the beast had to be preserved, by smoking, pickling or drying, as is done with pigs to this day. So knowledge of these procedures was necessary for a young bride, faced, for the first time, with a large, dead animal knowing it was up to her to make it 'Fitt for use until all was eaten.'

1. *To Pickle Grapes*

Take of your Grapes when fully growne but before they are Ripe and Putt them in your Potts.

Boyl a strong Brine and when Cold, throw it upon them.

2. To Pickle Barberrys

Take Barberrys when they be Ripe and Putt them into your Potts. Then take a strong Brine and Boyl in it some Cloves and ye washed Barberrys until it begins to look Red.

Then take it off ye ffire and, when it is cold, throw it on ye Barberrys.

The berries of this plant are said to relieve diarrhoea.

3. To Pickle Kidney Beans

Take Kidney Beans when Younge and lay them in Vinegar for a Week. Then Boyl them in water until they look Greene.

When they are Cold, lay them in your Potts and stir while strewing Peper, Cloves and Mace between them.

Then make a Pickle of water, Salt and Vinegar and throw it hott upon them.

4. To Pickle Oranges

Pare ye Oranges pretty Thicke and Hole. Boyl them in water until they are Tender for ye Pickle.

Boyl some water, take it off ye ffire and putt in a little Vinegar and Sugar according to your taste.

When it is cold, putt in your Oranges and keep them downe in it.

5. To Pickle Cowcombers

Take a Pint of White Wine Vinegar and Boyl it till it be one Quarter Consumed.

Then take it off ye ffire and Putt to it a goodly quantity of Salt. When it is thoroughly cold, wipe your Cowcombers very Clean, putt them into a Barrell or Pott and pour ye Liquor upon them.

When ye Pott is full, putt in a little good Oyl upon them and cover very Close.

When you eat them, take them out of ye Pickle, wipe them with a cloth and soe dishe them with Vinegar.

You may laye some bunches of Dill between them in ye Pott.

The green leaves of cucumber relieve dog bites. The seeds provoke urination and break up stone.

Applied externally, dill 'eases pain and heals tumours. The seed stops hiccups and vomiting. It stayeth the belly and is a gallant expeller of wind'. Most importantly, it protects against witchcraft.

6. To Pickle Stalks of Lettice or Purslane

Take of ye Fairest and largest Stalkes, cutt off ye Leaves and Boyl them in water till almost Tender for ye Pickle.

Then take them off ye ffire, putt them in Vinegar and a little Salt and keep them close covered.

Purslane, a salad ingredient, was said by William Cobbett to be eaten by 'pigs and by Frenchmen, when they can get nothing else'.

7. To Pickle Samphire

Picke your Samphire and putt it into ye Pott wherein you will Boyl it and press it down very Hard.

Then putt to it half White Wine Vinegar and half water (enough to Cover it). Sett it on ye ffire and lett it Boyl a little, but not too much, lest it growe softe.

Then take it off and lett it stand till Next Day. Then Heat it Scalding Hott and lett it cool again. If then it be not Greene enough, heat it once or twice more, till it comes to a good Colour.

Have a Care you do not Spoil it by Overheating.

Samphire grows on rocks by the sea, so would have been easy to find in the Dunleary area. It opens obstructions of the bowels, liver, spleen and kidneys, as well as stimulating the appetite if drunk in wine.

8. To Pickle Mushrooms

Take them and peal them and throwe them into fair water. Then take them up and putt them over a Soft ffire till they Boyl in their own Liquor a half Houre.

Then take them out of ye Liquor and putt some good Vinegar to it. Putt in some Cloves, Mace and Hole Peper and lett them Boyl a quarter Houre.

Keep your mushrooms till they be very cold and also your Liquor. Putt them together and soe lett them lie fourteen or fifteen days.

Then make a new Pickle for them of White Wine Vinegar.

'Mushrooms are of a cold, moist and crude nature, hurtful to the stomach if consumed in quantities.'

9. To Keep Quinces ye Year

Take some of ye Quinces Kernells and Corres and Boyl them well in as much water as will Cover them.

Then pour ye Liquor Hott upon ye Quinces, which must be hole and sound. Then cast Sugar into your Liquor and it will gather a thick Mother over it, which will preserve ye Quinces all year, Fitt for Pyes or Crame.

10. *To Preserve Cherrys*

Take one pound of Sugar, beaten fine to one pound of Cherrys. Stone and Boyl as many Cherrys as will yield about six or seven spoonfulls of Juice, in which you must dissolve your Sugar and Boyl up your Cherrys quick until you think they are almost (done) enough.

Take them from ye ffire and lett them stand a day or two, after which sett them on ye ffire and lett them Boyl softly until they are enough.

If you would preserve them in Jelly instead of the Juice of Cherrys, use ye Juice of Currans.

11. *To Preserve Cherrys Without Stone*

Stone your Cherrys, take their weight in refined Sugar and putt to it half a pint of Curran Liquor. Putt your Liquor on the Cherrys, with some of ye Sugar and sett it over ye ffire.

You must keep out most of your Sugar to throw in as they Boyl.

Lett them Boyl as fast as they can and when they are of a Carnation colour and Jellyd, they are enough.

Soe glass them up for your use.

12. To Preserve Damsons, Pears or Plumbs

To one pound of Plumbs, take one pound of Sugar Beaten. Throw a little Sugar in ye Bottom of a Silver Dishe, then Wipe ye Plumbs, slit them up ye seam and lay them one by one upon ye Sugar, ye Slit downwards.

Then Cover them over with some of ye other Sugar, sprinkle six spoonfulls of water upon them and sett them over a very smart ffire until you see some Sirrop coming from them and ye Sugar somewhat melted.

Cover them close and lett them stand two or three Houres.

After that, sett them over a quicke ffire and lett them melt your Sugar, strewing over the remainder of it when it is all Melted.

Lett them Boyl three Houres softly, then take them off ye ffire and cover them Close. Keep them by ye ffire all night.

Next day, Boyl them quicke and scum them clean. When ye Sirrop will stand, take it off ye ffire.

This method will also serve for Damsons or Pears.

13. How to Preserve Guesberrys or White Grapes

Cutt off ye Heads of your Guesberrys and to one Pound of them take one ounce of Refined Sugar and a half pint of water. With which make Sirrop and Boyl them in it gently for a While.

After this, Boyl them apace, soe that they may be covered with Sirrop. Then scum them.

When they are enough, they will look clear and Jellyd.

14. Another Way to Preserve Guesberrys

This is a quicke way but not as good. It may suffice for some.

To three pounds of refined Sugar putt about a quarter pint of water to dissolve it.

Then take half a pound of Guesberrys when they are full grown and before they are Ripe.

Cutt off their heads and Boyl them up quicke until they are clear.

15. To Preserve Aprycorkes in Jelly

Take Aprycorkes when almost Ripe, pare, stone and cutt them in halfs. Take to one pound of them one pound of refined Sugar. Putt them in a Bason, cover them with Sugar and soe lett them stand till ye next day. Then Boyl them till your Aprycorkes look Clear. Sett them by for three or four days. Then take half a pint of Pippin water and putt it to your Aprycorkes and Boyl them pretty Fast, still stiring it. When it is come to a Stiffe Jelly, take it off. It must look as clear as water and ye Aprycorkes a clear Yellow. It is best to preserve them in Halfes and to Boyl them one half upon another.

16. To Preserve Aprycorke Chips

Beat Sugar fine and sift it. Then take Aprycorkes before they be too ripe, peal and slice them very thin.

Then dipp them one by one in your Sugar and laye them on plates or dishes. Then sett them into your Oven. After one Houre, change them onto dry Plates (for Sirrop will have run from them which you may keep for other uses).

When you see 'tis time, turn them and be sure you change them often, for if you do not, they will eat Tuff. They must be kept dry.

17. To Candy Oranges or Lemmons

Take ye Oranges of Cevilla, pare or grate off ye outside Peal, cutt out a little peace with ye stem and with a Bodkin gently take out all ye seeds.

Wash ye Oranges and sett them on ye ffire in a great deal of water. Boyl them as fast as you can till they are tender, shifting them from one hott water to another till all the bitterness be gone.

Keep them covered, so no dust may get into them. Take a pound of Sugar and a pint of water, boil it to a Sirrop and scum it pretty clear. When it is cool, putt in a pound of your Boyled Oranges and lett them lye in it all night.

Next morning, make them just boyl and soe lett them stand a day or two longer. Then drain ye Sirrop from them and now Boyl it a little and soe pour it upon them again and lett them lye a day or two.

Then heat them as before and soe do two or three times until you see them look clean and ye Sirrop much wasted. Drain them as clean as you can from ye first Sirrop. Make a second Sirrop with about half ye weight of double refined Sugar just wet with water. Boyl and scum it clear.

Then putt in ye Oranges from ye other Sirrop. Boyl them to a Candy Height and then stop them. You must pick out ye Meat after they are Boyled.

Thus you may do them in halfs or little pieces as you like best.

18. To Preserve Oranges or Lemmons Hole

They must be done the same way as when Candied, which Receipt you have at hand, only with this addition.

When you have drained them from ye Sirrop ye last time, as here directed, take a pint of Pippin Jelly and a half pound of refined Sugar, boyld to a Candy Height. Putt your Pippin Jelly to them with ye Sirrop that was left in your Oranges, stiring it well together over ye ffire. But lett it not Boyl.

Putt your Oranges into several glasses and, when ye Jelly is cold, fill them up and putt ye stems you cutt off upon them.

Otherwise, you may defer putting them into ye Pippin Jelly until you use them and then you putt the juice of an Orange into it. But you must Boyl your Sirrop to a height that it may keep.

'Pippin jelly' (apple jelly) is also spelt pipen or pippen in the original.

19. To Dry Aprycorkes

Take half ye weight of ye Aprycorkes in Sugar, stone and pare them.

Then laye some Sugar in ye Bottom of your Pan. Upon them, laye your Aprycorkes and strew more Sugar over them. Soe lett them stand until ye Sugar be melted.

Then sett them over a good ffire and lett them Boyl as fast as a piece of Beefe till they be Tender.

Soe Lett them lye in Sirrop for two days. Then take them from it and laye them upon glass and dry them by the ffire.

20. To Preserve Wallnuts in ye Shells

Prick your Wallnuts full of holes with a great pin. Throw them into a posnett of Seething water and Boyl till tender, shifting them seven or eight times out of one Boyling into another.

You must not lett them Boyl or lye long in either of these waters, for it will make them look Blacke.

When they are tender, take them up and dry them in a clean cloth and stick into them a clove or two. Make a Sirrop of fine Sugar, as much as will cover them (you may putt in a grain of musk if you please) and Boyl them half an Houre softly. Take them up when your Sirrop is cold.

You may pott them and keep them all ye year.

21. To Preserve Green Fruits

Take your Greene plumbs in ye midst of July, sett two posnetts over ye ffire with water, ye first being scalding Hott. Putt ye plumbs in it, cover close and lett them stand a quarter Houre.

Then take them up with a spoon and putt them into ye other posnett, which must Boyl up and lett them stand in it half an houre.

Stir them about and take them up in a dishe and peal them as you do Coddlens. Then sett over another posnett of water and make it Boyl. Putt them into it and lett them stand until you see them look Greene.

Lett them simmer over ye ffire for a little while, not long for fear of Breaking. Soe take them up and weigh them with your Sugar and putt one ounce of Sugar above ye weight of Sugar and fruit.

Then sett a Dishe on a Chavendish on the coles and throw a little Sugar in ye Bottom of ye dishe.

Soe lay a Layering of plumes upon it and strew ye rest of your Sugar on ye top. Putt a little water into it and lett it Boyl till it be thicke.

Take them up and putt them into glasses for your Use. This way, beside Plumes, you may preserve Guesberrys or any Greene fruit.

A 'Chavendish' is a chafing dish.

22. To Candy Angelica

Take it while it is Young and Tender, putt it into cold water, cover it close and let it Boyl until it is very tender.

Take off ye peal and and string it and dry it very well in a cloth. Then weigh it and to every pound putt one and a quarter pounds of Loaf Sugar.

Throw some of your Sugar in ye Bottom of ye Preserving Pan. Then lay by turns, a laying of Angelica and a laying of Sugar until all be in. Add to it two spoonfulls of water and sett it aside till next day.

Ye next day, sett it over ye ffire, being close covered and lett it Boyl until ye Sirrop be pretty thick. Then take it out of ye Sirrop and lay it on a hurdle and dry very well by ye ffire or in ye wind.

When it be dry, take ye Sirrop and Clarify it with ye White of an Egge. When it be clear, add a quarter pound of double-refined Sugar and lett it Boyl up.

Take a spoonful of Gum Dragon, being steept in Rose Water, putt to it three or four spoonfuls of faire water and heat it a little together. Then putt it into your Sirrop and lett it boyl a little. Then putt in your Angelica and when it through it is done enough.

Soe lay it on your Hurdles and dry it as before.

Angelica is named after St Michael the Archangel because of an old legend. In a dream, Michael appeared to a monk and told him that Angelica could cure the plague. But that's not all. In the Middle Ages, parents used to dry and powder Angelica roots and give them to their children, mixed with wine 'to abate the raging lust in young persons'. Carrying a sprig of Angelica will avert witches' spells.

EPILOGUE

Although the Cannon family had spread far and wide during the generations that succeeded Patrick and Mary of Dunleary, there were always strong ties with Ireland. I was born in 1930 and have lived near Nenagh all my life, as my daughter and grandchildren still do. The book spans ten generations.

There were Cannons living in Dun Laoghaire (then Kingstown) until around 1900. Others had land in and around Balbriggan. The records are annoyingly sparse.

Rouquier Cannon and his son Aeneas travelled the world, but retired to Dublin, where Aeneas practised as a surgeon and where he married. His daughter Mary travelled uncomfortably in her crinoline, as described earlier, and must have been relieved when her husband, Charles Sloggett, retired from being an Army Chaplain and became rector of Chiddingfold, a peaceful English village.

One of her daughters, Gladys, married George Russell of High Park near Cappawhite in County Tipperary, while another lived in Ballydehob in County Cork. The family left High Park in 1910 and the place was bought by the Ryan family. As I write, it's for sale.

My mother came to live at Crannagh, near Nenagh, after her marriage to Standish Smithwick in 1929. Fifty years later to the day, she died in Nenagh Hospital. My daughter, Diana Fahey, lives at Crannagh now, with her husband Dan and their three children, Jack, Robyn and Luke.

Diana is an excellent cook, but I doubt if she plans to use Mary Cannon's recipes.